PHILOSOPHY:
CHRISTIAN PERSPECTIVES IN THE NEW MILLENNIUM

PHILOSOPHY:
CHRISTIAN PERSPECTIVES OF THE NEW MILLENNIUM

Editors:

Paul Copan
Scott B. Luley
Stan W. Wallace

Contributors Include:

Ravi Zacharias
Alister McGrath
J. P. Moreland
Stan W. Wallace
J. Budziszewski
Paul Copan
R. Douglas Geivett

Volume I
Philosophy: Christian Perspectives for the New Millenium

Copyright 2003 by
CLM & RZIM Publisher

CLM - Christian Leadership Ministries
www.clm.org
P. O. Box 129
Addison,TX 75001-0129
Phone: 972-713-7130 Fax: 972-713-7670
Email: clm@clm.org

RZIM - Ravi Zacharias International Ministries
www.rzim.org
4725 Peachtree Corners Circle Suite 250
Norcross, Georgia, 30092
Phone: 770-449-6766 Fax: 770-729-1729
Email: rzim@rzim.org

Bibliographical references and index
ISBN: 1-930107-19-6

1.Christianity - Philosophy

Printed in the United States of America
Editors Dr. Paul Copan, Dr. Scott Luley, Stan Wallace
First Printing, July 2003
Casebound Edition

PHILOSOPHY:
CHRISTIAN PERSPECTIVES
OF THE NEW MILLENNIUM

Paul Copan, Scott B. Luley, and Stan W. Wallace – Editors
CLM/RZIM Publishers

DEDICATION 7

ACKNOWLEDGMENTS 9

INTRODUCTION 11

Part I: Context and Strategies

1. THE BATTLE FOR IDEAS 19
      Dr. Ravi Zacharias
      President, Ravi Zacharias International Ministries

2. WORLDVIEWS IN CONFLICT 33
      Dr. Alister McGrath
      Professor of Historical Theology, Oxford University, England

3. ACADEMIC INTEGRATION AND CHRISTIAN SCHOLARSHIP 59
      Dr. J. P. Moreland
      Professor of Philosophy, Talbot School of Theology

4. ESSENTIALS OF POSTMODERNISM .75
    Stan W. Wallace
    Coordinator, Emerging Scholars Network and Gulf States
    Area Director InterVarsity Christian Fellowship Graduate
    and Faculty Ministries

Part II: Philosophical Responses to Current Challenges

5. PRACTICAL RESPONSES TO RELATIVISM
   AND POSTMODERNISM: PART I 89
    Dr. J. Budziszewski
    Assoc. Professor of Government & Philosophy,
    The University of Texas, Austin

6. PRACTICAL RESPONSES TO RELATIVISM
   AND POSTMODERNISM: PART II (WITH DISCUSSION) 107
    Dr. J. Budziszewski
    Assoc. Professor of Government & Philosophy,
    The University of Texas, Austin

7. HOW CAN A GOOD GOD ALLOW EVIL AND SUFFERING?   . .123
    Dr. R. Douglas Geivett
    Professor of Philosophy, Talbot School of Theology
    at Biola University

8. HUMAN NATURE AND THE SEARCH FOR GOD 149
    Dr. Paul Copan
    Lecturer and Author, Ravi Zacharias International
    Ministries and Visiting Associate Professor, Trinity
    International University

DEDICATION

*"The philosophy of the classroom in one generation
will be the philosophy of society in the next generation."*

This book project is dedicated to two groups of people seeking to change society in the next generation by influencing the philosophy of the classroom in this generation.

The *first group* includes courageous Christian men and women who seek to integrate their faith and scholarship in the university. As forerunners, these scholars provide articulate "expression" so others can find evidence for a Christian worldview in any discipline.

The *second group* includes the staff of our respective ministries—*Christian Leadership Ministries* (CLM) and *Ravi Zacharias International Ministries* (RZIM). Every person serving with our respective ministries contributed to making this international conference a success.

At the time of the conference, the CLM staff were:

Byron & Dianne Barlowe	*Dr. Walter & Ann Bradley*
*Dan & Tricia Clement**	*Jim & Phyllis Cook*
Dr. William Lane & Jan Craig	*Peter & Patti Culver*
Kent & Denise Dahlberg	*Dave & Janet DeHuff*
Paula Dorough	*Mike & Susie Duggins*
Jim & Brenda Dunn	*John & Connie Engberg*
Steve & Wanda Faivre	*Dr. Geri Forsberg & Paul Madison*
*Larry & Teresa Freeman**	*Paul & Noelle Gebel*
Dr. Ray & JoAnn Goforth	*Paul & Ethel Gould**
Bill & Jan Hager	*Dr. Pattie Harris*
Paul & Judy Hartgrove	*Don & Linda Hayes**
Gary & Gena Hellman	*Jim Huston*
Mark & Maureen Jacus	*Howie & Nance Kauffman*
Randy & Mary Gayle Kennedy	*Frank & Judy Kifer*

* indicates those who joined CLM staff since the conference.

7

Ken & Frances Knutzen
Randy & Cheryl Lee
Phil & Kay Luther
John & Sandy Mackin
Rich & Bonnie McGee
Kaye Merritt*
John & Cathy Myers
Randy & Pam Newman
Steve & Sarah Pogue
Patrick & Rachel Rist
Keith & Kay Seabourn
Harold & Presha Simmons
Steve & Betsy Sternberg
Dave & Polly Thom
Dr. John & Pat Walkup
Scott & Cathy Waller
Dave & Beth Wiley

Glen & Barbara Leckman
Dr. Scott & Jan Luley
Charlie & Chrissie Mack
Dr. Mike & Lisa Madaris
Dr. Rae & Peggy Mellichamp
Joe & Jane Mulvihill
Dr. Dave & Karen Ness
Chris & Sharon Peck*
Dave & Pam Richardson
Dr. Chuck & Dianne Roeper
Bob & Jeannette Schroer
Mike & Lee Anne Sorgius
Dennis & Norma Suchecki
Howard & Debbie Van Cleave
Stan & Lori Wallace
Dr. Jim & Anne Wenger
Daryl & Ceil Wilson

At the time of the conference, the RZIM staff were:

Malcolm Armstrong
Dolores Barfield
Merrilee Carlson
George Curry
Danielle DuRant
Ryan Hayward
Peggy Lasseter
Bea Maxfield
Alistair McPherson
Travis Poortinga
Erik Rowe
Bill Smith
Linda Wolfe
Nathan Zacharias

Scott Armstrong
Nancy Bevers
Rhonda Caudell
Penny DeHaan
Dan Glaze
Mary Holman
Paul Lundblad
Mary McAllister
Gordon Moore
Laura Reinert
Kara Sanford
Steve Unwin
Margie Zacharias
Ravi Zacharias

Helen Barclay
Bonnie Canaday
Paul Copan
Gavin Douglas
Harriett Guinn
Eric Hunter
Matt Martz
Stuart McAllister
Joshua Moore
Andy Rhodes
Becky Schulz
Mark Veerman
Naomi Zacharias

CLM, the faculty ministry of Campus Crusade for Christ, reaches out to and through professors and future professors at secular universities to *win* them to faith in Jesus Christ, *build* them in their faith, and *send* them to influence others on campuses in the United States and around the world.

RZIM seeks to reach and challenge those who shape the ideas of culture with the credibility and the beauty of the Gospel of Jesus Christ through evangelism, apologetics, spiritual disciplines, and training.

ACKNOWLEDGMENTS

—⁊⁊⁊—

It has been a pleasure for us to work together on this multi-book project. Our partnership began as we served together on the Program Committee for the *God and the Academy Conference*, which was co-hosted by our ministries (CLM and RZIM).

We acknowledge all who designed and implemented the *God and the Academy Conference* which this book documents. It was a team effort by both ministries.

Special thanks to several people who contributed significantly to this book series. Deirdre Boyer and Steve Hollaway helped in many different ways throughout the publishing process. Ryan Bonfiglio, a Princeton University graduate, gave valuable feedback on how each volume's essays could best reach the target audience we chose. Alison Lentini and Tricia Clement gave editorial advice and LeeAnne Sorgius, Anna McCarroll, and Deirdre Boyer transcribed many audiotapes of the conference lectures into manuscripts for editing.

We acknowledge the founding members of CLM's Academic Initiative Executive Committee—Bob Schroer, Patrick Rist, Randy Newman and Scott Waller—for their help in planning and helping direct the *God and the Academy Conference* program. These men are exemplars of scholar-activists who deeply love both Christ and the academy.

We acknowledge the contributions of three RZIM staff—Gordon Moore, Sarah Davis, and Joshua Moore, all who accepted the task of formatting the volumes in our series. Sarah Davis joined RZIM after the conference, but gave valuable input and support to this co-publishing venture of CLM and RZIM.

Projects of this magnitude always require the support of family and co-workers. We acknowledge their commitment to Jesus Christ and His desire to "seek and speak" to those for whom this book is written.

PAUL COPAN, PH.D.

*Lecturer and Author, Ravi Zacharias International Ministries and
Visiting Associate Professor, Trinity International University*

Paul Copan has studied at Columbia Bible College (B.A.), Trinity Evangelical Divinity School (M.A., Philosophy of Religion; M.Div.), and Marquette University (Milwaukee), where he received his Ph.D. in philosophy. He is a Visiting Assistant Professor at Trinity Evangelical Divinity School. He has co-authored and written several books and is currently ministry associate with RZIM. He currently resides in Suwanee, GA with his wife Jacqueline and their five children

SCOTT LULEY, PH.D.

*Director, Christian Leadership Ministries at Princeton University
& the Eastern US Region*

Scott Luley earned his B.S. degree from Lehigh University and his M.B.A. and Ph.D. degrees from Penn State University. In 1980 he helped to found Christian Leadership Ministries. Dr. Luley is currently Director of Christian Leadership Ministries at Princeton University and in the Eastern US Region. He lives near Princeton University with his wife Jan and two teenage boys.

STAN W. WALLACE, M.A

*Coordinator, Emerging Scholars Network and Gulf States Area Director
InterVarsity Christian Fellowship Graduate and Faculty Ministries*

Stan Wallace earned his B.S. in Education from Miami University, his M.A. in Philosophy of Religion and Ethics from Talbot School of Theology, and has pursued doctoral studies in Philosophy at Marquette University. He is currently Coordinator of the Emerging Scholars Network and serves as an Area Director with Intervarsity Christian Fellowship's Graduate and Faculty Ministries. Stan lives in Tampa, Florida with his wife Lori and four children.

INTRODUCTION

———ᴗᴗᴗ———

We live in an era called "postmodern." Today, the term is overused, but it accurately describes the skeptical responses and rejection of objective truth claims—especially those proposing answers to life's most important and ultimate questions. Today, many "modernist" systems (Enlightenment rationalism, Marxism, and/or Nazism) have failed to deliver their utopian promises, leaving many to wonder if all that is left are the idiosyncratic beliefs of individuals and social groups. We are told this is the postmodern mindset.

One pervasive and influential worldview in our contemporary culture seeking to offer a comprehensive explanation of the way things are is scientific naturalism. It claims all that exists and can be experienced must be explained only in terms of natural, as opposed to supernatural, causes.

Our current culture provides a mixed bag of approaches to truth, knowledge, life, meaning, and purpose. Christians in any sector of society are confronted by challenges to the Gospel and revelation—in any form— by skeptics of truth claims as they are urged to adopt a secular worldview.

To deal with challenges like these, Ravi Zacharias International Ministries and Christian Leadership Ministries partnered together to sponsor *God and the Academy: Charting a Course for the New Millennium.* This was a conference international in scope and designed to bring together Christians who recognize the "culture-shaping" influence of education—particularly in the secular university. The conference was held at the Georgia Institute of Technology in June 2000.

Charles Malik, former President of the United Nations General Assembly, proposed "two tasks" for higher education—one spiritual and the other intellectual, saving the soul and saving the mind.

All the preaching in the world, and all the loving care of even the best parents between whom there are no problems whatever, will amount to little, if not to nothing, so long as what the children are exposed to day in and day out for fifteen to twenty years in the school and university virtually cancels out, morally and spiritually, what they hear and see and learn at home and in the church.[1]

As Christians, we are called to evangelism, but also to engage education in a dialogue that challenges the reigning the assumptions and ideas underlying our postmodern culture.

In 1913, the President of Princeton Seminary, J. Gresham Machen, expressed this same vision with words that ring as true today as they did then:

> We may preach with all the fervor of a reformer and
> yet succeed only in winning a straggler here and there,
> if we permit the whole collective thought of the
> nation to be controlled by ideas that, by the resistless
> force of logic, prevent Christianity from being regarded
> as anything more than a harmless delusion.[2]

To this end, we offer the following volumes to "capture" the ideas proposed and discussed at the conference our ministries co-sponsored:

Philosophy: Christian Perspectives of the New Millennium
Science: Christian Perspectives of the New Millennium

These volumes are designed to (1) help believers think Christianly about a wide array of topics, and (2) offer ideas and dialogue to those outside the Christian community who often have legitimate questions about the Gospel. We feel there is more than enough evidence to challenge any serious skeptic who understands that God never minds serious questions—only the insult of being ignored.

Jeremiah wrote in the Old Testament,

> Thus says the Lord, "Let not a wise man boast of his
> wisdom, and let not the mighty man boast of his
> might, let not a rich man boast of his riches; but let
> him who boasts boast of this, that he understands and
> knows Me, that I am the Lord who exercises
> lovingkindness, justice, and righteousness on earth; for
> I delight in these things," declares the Lord (9:23-24).

As co-editors, we are committed to the integration of faith and learning in education. Our lives, ministries, and these volumes reflect a commitment to advance the cause of Christ by presenting a Christian worldview in secular universities. That viewpoint is often marginalized in the university community. To address this situation, great effort has been exerted to design this book to reflect the issues thinking Christians everywhere often discuss. As editors, we have done this in several ways.

First, we chose *authors* who are currently some of the best thinkers within the Christian community—most are professors at prominent secular universities. Second, we chose *topics* that are at the center of debate in secular universities and society in general. Third, we included "give and take" audience *discussions* from the same or a similar lecture given at a prominent secular university. These lectures and audience discussions are very helpful as they reveal what many students today think, feel, and believe. We are committed to the inclusion of such material, as it can prevent our "talking to ourselves." These volumes reflect a sincere attempt to engage the academy and culture of our time.

This philosophy volume is divided into two parts. *Part I* offers a context and strategy for philosophical engagement in the academy. The lead essay comes from philosopher and lecturer *Ravi Zacharias*, who speaks of the "battle of ideas" in the academy. He points out the arrogance of certain scientists who seek to reduce human life and meaning to physics and chemistry. He shows how critics in academia denounce Christianity because of abuses committed in the name of Christ, yet these critics themselves tend to be moral relativists. Furthermore, while there is an alleged openness to "spirituality" at the university, the supernatural—and specifically the Christian faith—is denied.

Theologian *Alister McGrath* ("Worldviews in Conflict") introduces us to the importance of Christian apologetics in a postmodern world. He examines how St. Paul defends the gospel in the book of Acts, and he notes how two apologists of the 20th century—C. S. Lewis and Francis Schaeffer—carried out an apologetic so effectively. Philosopher *J. P. Moreland*'s essay ("Academic Integration and Christian Scholarship") describes the relation between integration and spiritual formation; he goes on to discuss current integrative priorities for the Christian scholar; and then he analyzes the epistemic tasks for and models employed in integration. The last essay of this section ("Essentials of Postmodernism") by philosopher *Stan W. Wallace* outlines two key features to postmodernism—(a) the acceptance of nominalism, which is the rejection of universals, and (b) the rejection of truth as correspondence. These are vitally important matters, and one must understand them in order to think Christianly about postmodernism.

Part II deals with philosophical responses to current challenges. In the first two chapters of this section ("Practical Responses to Relativism and Postmodernism," Parts I and II), philosopher *J. Budziszewski* confronts many of the incoherencies of postmodernism and relativism (including an engaging audience discussion). Ultimately, human beings cannot escape truth or the moral law that God has placed within us. As Christians, we must utilize strategies that both affirm the person and expose the hollowness of relativism. Philosopher *Douglas Geivett* offers an important treatment of the problem of evil. He tackles important questions such as: How is evil to be defined? What are the different types of problems (e.g., the intellectual and the existential)? Is the co-existence of God and evil logically contradictory? Even if it is not, why would God allow so much evil in the world? In the final essay ("Human Nature and the Search for God"), philosopher *Paul Copan* speaks of how human nature reflects and points us to the divine. If a Creator exists, then we are not surprised to discover that the universe is finite and had a beginning (the Big Bang) and is astonishingly fine-tuned for life. And if human beings have been made in the image of God, then we are not surprised to that we have the features we do: personality, dignity and worth; rationality; self-awareness; a moral constitution; and the capacity to make free, responsible choices. The existence of a good and powerful Creator better explains such features, as opposed to naturalism, in which human beings emerge from impersonal, worthless, unguided, non-conscious, non-moral, deterministic processes. Theism offers a more plausible context for such characteristics than does naturalism.

We hope that the contributions to this volume on philosophy and the Christian worldview—along with its companion volume on science and the Christian worldview—will serve to equip, stimulate, and challenge its readers.

Paul Copan, Ph.D.
> *Ravi Zacharias International Ministries*
> *Trinity International University*

Scott Luley, Ph.D.
> *Director, Christian Leadership Ministries at Princeton University*
> *& the Eastern US Region*

Stan W. Wallace, M.A
> *Coordinator, Emerging Scholars Network and Gulf States Area Director*
> *InterVarsity Christian Fellowship Graduate and Faculty Ministries*

---

[1] Charles Malik, *The Two Tasks* (Westchester, Ill.: Crossway, 1980), 27.
[2] "Christianity and Culture," *Princeton Theological Review* 11 (1913): 7.

PART I:

CONTEXT AND STRATEGIES

Chapter One

—⟪⟫—

THE BATTLE OF IDEAS

Ravi Zacharias

Dr. Ravi Zacharias is president of Ravi Zacharias International Ministries in Norcross, Georgia. He is an internationally-respected speaker and author. He has written several books, including Can Man Live Without God? (Word), Jesus Among Other Gods (Word), and The Lotus and the Cross (Multnomah).

Abstract

"If there is one apologetic struggle I live with, it is this question: Why is it so many people who talk of a supernatural transformation show so little of the transformed life? Why, when we talk so much about the regenerating work of the Holy Spirit, is it no longer so obvious to the unbeliever, who fails to see the change, but only hears our language?"

Lostness wears many different faces, and as we consider the academy, where there is a celebration of the mind and the intellect, we find it is becoming harder to understand how to bring the simple truths of the gospel into such an arena.

A few years ago, Paul Johnson, the English historian, wrote a book called *The Intellectuals*; it received mixed reviews, but in the closing statement in the book, he ends with these lines, "Above all we must remember at all times what intellectuals habitually forget: that people matter more than concepts and must come first. The worst of all despotisms is the heartless tyranny of ideas."[1]

The June 2000 issue of the *Atlantic Monthly* included an article called "Harvard and the Makings of the Unabomber," by Dr. Alston Chase.[2] Chase traces the journey from intellectual optimism to intellectual despair in Ted Kaczynski. He has some marvelous insights into what actually happened. In his closing paragraphs Chase makes this comment:

> The real story of Ted Kaczynski is one of the nature of modern evil—evil that results from the corrosive powers of intellect itself, and its arrogant tendency to put ideas above common humanity and by this process of abstraction to dehumanize our enemies.

Chase goes on to talk about the experiments to which Kaczynski was subjected—the Murray experiment—which he describes in these words: "'vehement, sweeping, and personally abusive' attacks, assaulting his subjects' egos and most-cherished ideals and beliefs."

I would like us to understand and accept not only the face of the attack, but the heart of the battle. In doing this, we can get to the truth and not lose sight of the person.

An Unblushing Stridency and a Smuggled-in Autocracy

The *first* and foremost challenge is the face that stands before us in the academy—a face which is *unblushingly strident* and exhibits *a smuggled-in autocracy.* Once upon a time, the ramifications of anti-theism or atheism or agnosticism were at least understood for what they were. For example, when you read Darwin's explanation of evolution, he notes that the moral and philosophical ramifications of this idea could be dire.[3] He shuddered at the possibility of how "nature red in tooth and claw" could engender horrific carnage in the years, decades, and centuries to come. Darwin understood the logical implications of the worldview that would be engendered from his theory. He was fearful of what its possibilities would entail. Even Nietzsche, as bold and unapologetic as he was, realized the entailments that flow from God's being dead and our being autonomous. The moral playing field is stripped wide open, and the consequences could be staggering if carried to their logical conclusions.

Once upon a time, the naturalist, understanding his worldview, had a healthy respect for these Nietzschean possibilities. And with some degree of apprehension, he would try to work his way through them. While naturalists have regularly and roundly attacked cosmological and design arguments for God's existence, now all of a sudden the moral argument is the one that is now also facing a significant challenge. With this challenge comes a fearsome stridency.

For instance, listen to the words of Richard Dawkins illustrating the philosophical ramifications of naturalism:

> . . . there was a well-known television chef who did a stunt recently by cooking a human placenta and serving it up as a pate, fried with shallots, garlic, lime juice, and everything. Everybody said it was delicious. The father had 17 helpings. A scientist can point out, as I have done, that this is actually an act of cannibalism. Worse, since cloning is such a live issue at the moment, because the placenta is a true genetic clone of the baby . . . . Science can't tell you if it's right or wrong to eat your own baby's clone, but it can tell you that's what

you're doing, then you can decide for yourself whether
you think it's right or wrong.[4]

On one hand, Dawkins declares that science cannot tell you
whether what you are doing is right or wrong. On the other, science has
the authority to tell you that you alone determine whether it is right or
wrong.

New York University philosopher Thomas Nagel exemplifies the
strident resistance to God typical of many academics. He frankly admits:

> In speaking of the fear of religion, I don't mean to refer
> to the entirely reasonable hostility toward certain
> established religions…in virtue of their objectionable
> moral doctrines, social policies and political influence.
> Nor am I referring to the association of many religious
> beliefs with superstition and the acceptance of evident
> empirical falsehoods. I am talking about something
> much deeper—namely the fear of religion itself I
> want atheism to be true and am made uneasy by the
> fact that some of the most intelligent and well-
> informed people I know are religious believers. It isn't
> just that I don't believe in God and, naturally, hope
> there is no God! I don't want there to be a God; I don't
> want the universe to be like that.[5]

Not only do we see an *unblushing stridency,* we also see a
smuggled-in autocracy. For example, many in the academy attempt to
reduce all explanations to chemistry, biology, or physics. If such a
reductionism were true, then these scientists could claim that they have
explanatory power over all of life itself.

When I finished an open forum at Cornell University, packed with
over a thousand students, a young woman came to the front and was
literally crying. She said, "Every waking moment I am living with
naturalistic assumptions. You are presenting an ultimate paradigm shift.
How can I possibly make that kind of a change in the atmosphere in
which I am living every waking moment of my life?" One can pity her
deep struggle: Why can't physics explain it all?

Listen again to Dawkins: "There is at the bottom of it all no good, no evil, no purpose, nothing but [and note the value-added term] blind pitiless indifference. DNA neither knows nor cares. DNA just is, and we dance to its music."[6] According to Dawkins and his ilk, we can all be reduced somehow to physics or chemistry or biology. There is a smuggled-in autocracy in such a sweeping, comprehensive reductionism.

Pointing out the Immoral While Undermining Morality

There is a *second* challenge: *A disposition that points out the immoral while de-legitimizing morality at the same time.* I don't know if I've been in an open forum anywhere when there has not been a student or a professor from somewhere who has stood up and talked about all of the atrocities that have been committed in the name of Christianity. It is not just in the West that you hear this. You can travel to any Middle Eastern country, where Muslims will tell you this as well. I hear it in India time and time again. The truth of the matter was aptly summed up by Mahatma Ghandi, when asked about the Christian faith: "I like their Christ, and I don't like their Christians."[7]

A survey of the historical record shows many atrocities and misdeeds done in the name of Christ, and these are a black eye in the face of Christendom, and we must own up to these tragedies. Academics are quick to point out *immoral acts* done in the name of God, but where does atheism potentially lead us? To the de-legitimization of objective morality.

However, there is a difference between such misdeeds within Christendom and those done in the name of atheism, which has in its politicized exploits, in point of fact, engendered greater carnage than "Christendom." Indeed, when atheism has worked its way into violence and sensuality, it was the *logical* outworking of many tenets of the atheistic worldview, which offer no foundation for human dignity or human rights. Yet when politicized Christianity did what it did, it was in *violation* of the teaching and the very person of Christ. The difference is in the worldviews.

What is more, the matter expresses itself beyond the intellectual and penetrates the personal. Perhaps somewhere within the recesses of the human heart, we may not be battling intellectual ideas so much as the right to express personal preferences—our sexual proclivities and passionate indulgences. Aldous Huxley expressed this in his book *Ends and Means*: "We objected to morality because it interfered with our sexual freedom."[8] God may simply be that which stands in the way of my unfettered autonomy and the expression of my desires.

You and I have normal drives, but how much more perverse can your passions be when you want the freedom to do whatever you want to do whenever you want to do it in any way you want to do it? At least in the temptations common to us all, the Christian leans upon the power of God to resist. The anti-theist may want to be rid of God for the sake of unbridled freedom and sexuality. Although this does not disprove the atheist's position, it is important to consider what may be the very heart of his struggle.

After one of my university lectures with well over 1,000 in attendance, a woman ran up, grabbed the microphone, and screamed out at me: "Who told *you* life needed to be coherent? Where did you get this idea of cultural coherence from?"

I replied, "Wait a minute, ma'am. I was quoting sociologist Daniel Bell, who said culture is an effort to find a coherent set of answers for the existential questions that confront all of us in the passage of our lives."

She said, "Ah! Words, words, words."

I replied, "All right, I will try to answer you, but I have one question for you first: Do you want my answer to you to be *coherent*, or may it be incoherent?"

Although much happened that night, the sad reality emerged after the talk when I was being driven back to the airport the next day. One of the organizers asked, "Are you aware of the person who raised that question?" I said, "No I'm not." He explained that the physical body of that particular questioner was itself a contradiction—supposedly born one way, but hormonally predisposed another.

One wonders why she would want a coherent set of answers to life if her body itself was sending incoherent signals to her. My heart was heavy with the realization of what she was probably battling.

The academy today rails against the immoral actions among professing believers—while through the back door it is smuggling in an epistemology based on physiology at worst and moral relativism at best.

Promoting Spirituality While Denying the Supernatural

We saw, first, an unblushing stridency with a smuggled-in autocracy; then we noted a disposition that points out the immoral while undermining morality. The *third challenge is a language that endorses spirituality, while intellectually it denies the spiritual or the supernatural.*

On campuses we get a heavy dose of spirituality. One is welcome to talk freely about Eastern philosophies such as Buddhism, Hinduism, or some pantheistic worldview. And that's fine, for I think in a legitimately pluralistic society, we must be able to hear these counter-perspectives and people be given freedom to share those views.

My heartache, however, is this: *Why are these views accepted with cultural protection, while the Christian faith is openly debunked and mocked?* We commonly hear a language that endorses spirituality, while intellectually denying the supernatural—and the Christian faith in particular.

But even this is only the façade. The chief ideas being brought in through the back door are a divinization of the counter-culture and the deification of the self.

Let me try to pull this down into a funnel point here so that I can offer three different responses to this predicament. If you turn to Hindu scriptures such as the Upanishads, you will read of a father talking to his son, who had gone away for twelve years to obtain an education. However, he still fails to grasp what the self is really all about. So the father decides to teach the son. We read of their conversation in one particular Upanishad—the Chandogya.

The father looks at the son and points to a tree and says, "Bring me a fruit from the banyan tree."

The son says, "Here it is, father."

The father says, "Break this fruit open."

The son does so.

Then the father says, "What do you see now?"

He replies, "I see very small seeds."

"Break open one of those seeds."

"It is broken, sir."

"What do you see in it?"

And the son says, "I see nothing—absolutely nothing."

The father looks at him and says, "My son, from the very essence in the seed which you cannot see comes this vast banyan tree. Out of such nothingness, son, sprouts your life." Then he gives his son famous line from Upanishadic teaching: "*Tat tvam asi*. Thou art that—*nothingness*."⁹ In other words, nothingness is your essential nature. Out of this nothingness emerges your flowering individuality.

Incidentally, this is true not just in Eastern philosophy but in science. It is fascinating that while science has advanced so far—and now philosophers are pleading that we must have an interest in people, not just in ideas—the truth of the matter is that *the value of the person is lost*.

When you escape into Eastern philosophy, you find there some marriage of the minds with some Western academics. There is an essence of nothing in the essential self. You end up with some kind of a fluid idea of Ultimate Reality, which then ultimately goes and is in the end absorbed into that impersonal Absolute (called *Brahman*), and the self no longer exists as we know it.

One fundamental difference between the gospel of Christ and the pantheistic worldview is this: Jesus identified the *individual* so clearly and called upon that individual for communion with the divine in an "I-You" relationship whereas Eastern pantheism eradicates that individuality. That's why in Eastern pantheism, there is only one capital *I* and no "I-You." The self is lost. What results in the effort to exalt an autocratic or autonomous self is a society in which the self has no value at all. Little wonder that a man like Ted Kaczynski did not think that he was killing any *people*—he was only killing an *idea!*

Three Responses to the Current Situation

What can you and I do in this situation? I give you three suggestions to deal with this unblushing stridency; to this disposition that points to the immoral while simultaneously undermining the moral; and to this language that endorses spirituality while intellectually denying the supernatural.

First, *if the heart of the battle is the struggle to anchor morality, then for the Christian, life must be inseparable from the Word.* If there is one apologetic struggle I live with, it is this question: *Why is it so many people who talk of a supernatural transformation show so little of the transformed life?* Why, when we talk so much about the regenerating work of the Holy Spirit, is it no longer so obvious to the unbeliever, who fails to see the change, but only hears our language?

Somehow, we in the academy must come to grips with the possibility that we no longer need to convince the average student of the aimlessness with which the majority of people live. But somewhere that student may desperately need to see a life that is consistently lived in its proclamation and in its deed.

Consider Sir Thomas More in *A Man For All Seasons*, when he was imprisoned for not supporting his king in an immoral venture. His daughter comes to him and says, "Father, why don't you at least *in words* approve of the king's actions? You don't have to really mean it in your heart. Just verbally affirm what the king is doing. Then we can have you back. They will let you out of this prison."

Sir Thomas More looks at his daughter and says, "Meg, you don't understand! You don't understand what one's *word* means." He said, "When you give somebody your word, it is like taking your life and holding it—cupping it—in your hands. And should you let that word fall through, you will look down and not find yourself there."

If there is something the secular world longs to see, it is that the *life* of the Christian apologist, philosopher, economist, mathematician, scientist—or whatever discipline you come from, my brother and my sister—manifests an attractive, transformed inner quality. Then as they are enchanted by the brilliance of the mind that God has so mercifully given to you, they will see the translation of it into a humble spirit—a life that is so beautifully lived.

Henri Nouwen, who wrote *The Return of the Prodigal Son*,[10] gave up his teaching position at Harvard in order to work with the mentally handicapped in Toronto. His book was based on the power Rembrandt's painting *The Return of the Prodigal Son* had upon his life when he had gone to St. Petersburg and stared at that picture for three hours. Henri Nouwen said to himself: "I have preached an awful lot about the forgiving father, the receiving father. I'm not sure I have fully been engulfed in that myself to understand this kind of love." He said he went to work with the mentally handicapped "not because I had something to teach them, but because they had something to teach me."

He wrote of one of the young women at the institution who would always stand at the door welcoming each new person, who might have saliva dribbling from the mouth. But she would just reach over and grab them and embrace them, give them a kiss and welcome them into that place. Henri Nouwen said, "It had been a long time since I understood what it was to receive such unconditional love."

Secondly, hope is to be inseparable from death. As we talk about the hope for the university and all its possibilities, my plea is this: We must always bear in mind that God not only wants us to proclaim the triumphs and the victory that He gives, but also—and here's what I want to say to you as candidly as I can—*never to forget the heart of the gospel, which is the cross of Jesus Christ.*

Mahatma Gandhi said it clearly. There are many things in the Vedas he wished he could remove; there are many things about the Christian faith he did not understand—and some he did not like. But the most powerful truth in the Christian gospel is unmatched anywhere else—the cross of Jesus Christ. Even Martin Luther King, Jr., in one of the most colorful sermons he ever preached, declared the marvel and the beauty of the cross. If we forget that, we have forgotten the heart of the gospel.

The director of an interdisciplinary study of religion and science in England has pleaded with the church to change:

> To be truly "evangelical" and "catholic," the church of
> the next millennium will need a theology that will
> necessarily have to be genuinely liberal and even radical—
> particularly in its relation to a worldview everywhere
> shaped by the sciences. For Christian theology to have

any viability, it may well have to be stripped down to newly-conceived essentials, minimalist in its affirmations. Only then will it attain that degree of verisimilitude with respect to *ultimate* realities which science has to *natural* ones—and command respect as a vehicle of public truth.[11]

I've got news for this scholar: what he wants is a Christianity that is not evidently biblical—namely, a theology ever-informed by, and never informing, science.

When I speak at open forums in universities worldwide, the greatest silence in the audience comes in the last 20 minutes of two days of presentations, when I take them back to the cross before taking them to the empty tomb. And as that cross is expounded, there is silence in the auditorium as the hearts of men and women are listening eagerly to this counter-perspective of Jesus Christ that stands so unique and so awesomely powerful. The cross—rather than the theological minimalism I just cited—has the capacity to captivate hearts in our society.

Lastly, the struggle is inseparable from the triumph. These are indeed hard days. But I also believe that somehow in the midst of all of this, God is still going to bring some triumph of glorious possibilities.

Some years ago I was in Beirut, Lebanon, where I have a friend called Sammy. He is a short man—and like a teddy bear, just bursting with enjoyment and cheer. He loves doctrine, and he loves life—and he loves to live out that doctrine. You can never talk anything in silence or quietude with him. He's loud. You sit in his van, and it moves more by prayer than by any mechanical ability under that hood. He drives you through enemy territory with the bumper sticker, "Man shall not live by bread alone, but by every word that proceeds from the mouth of God."

As we were chugging along one day, some Syrian soldiers—all armed to the teeth—stopped us. I thought, "That's it. I'll be buried in the Beka Valley." They asked us to lower the window, and an officer planted his gun into the van. He looked at Sammy and said, "Do you have any dynamite? Any explosives?"

Sammy said, "Yes! This van is full of explosives!"

I was sitting next to him, thinking, "This guy is strange. I don't know where he gets this humor from."

Then Sammy rummaged under a tarpaulin over the van, with the Syrian soldiers just staring at him, and he pulled out a New Testament, and he says, "This is the dynamite. It's not the kind that will hurt."

The Syrian soldier was rather disgusted with that. Sammy insisted that he take it; so the soldier decided to pay attention to me. After remarking on my status as an Indian, he saluted us again and waved us on.

Sammy drove on for about twenty yards and pulled up. I asked myself, "Now what is he doing?"

He looked at me and said, "Brother Ravi, you don't know how much it upsets me to see all these soldiers—50,000 of them—from another land, taking over my country. One day I got on my knees. I was angry with God, and I asked him what he was doing to my land, sending all these people in here. And I sensed God interrupting me, saying, 'Sammy, just a minute. For all these years you have complained that Syria has not allowed missionaries within her territory, and you kept complaining that I do something about it. And now that I sent 50,000 Syrians to you, you are still complaining about it.'"

Ladies and gentlemen, God has placed *you* in the academy. He is giving you an audience that will make a world of a difference some day—even if you are facing stiff challenges and difficulties.

Let me close with this simple illustration. I've been to Athens many times. When I was there last, and I noticed something I had never noticed before. We had just come off Mars Hill, and I was walking on the main street by Mars Hill and the Areopagus there. It's a beautiful setting with a magnificent history. As we were walking on that street, I suddenly caught sight of the road sign. The name of the street—I couldn't believe what I was reading. So I called all of my friends together and said, "Look at that name on this road opposite Mars Hill. Look at this big street; look at what it is called: "*Dionysios ho Areopagitēs*"— Dionysius the Areopagite. When Paul went to Athens, the Bible says some scoffed; some said they would hear him another time; and some of them believed. One of them was Dionysius the Areopagite. Two thousands years later, the street bears his name.

Someday, somewhere, a great mind will be proclaiming the gospel for Christ's sake. Behind it may well be your name because you stood firm and you stood strong. My heart is burdened for the academy, and how glad I am that men and women like you are there. May God richly bless you.

---

1 Paul Johnson, *Intellectuals* (New York: Harper & Row, 1988), 342.

2 *Atlantic Monthly* 285/6 (June 2000). See http://www.theatlantic.com/issues/2000/06/chase.htm).

3 For instance, Darwin mused:

> If, for instance, to take an extreme case, men were reared under precisely the same conditions as hive-bees, there can hardly be a doubt that our unmarried females would, like the worker-bees, think it a sacred duty to kill their brothers, and mothers would strive to kill their fertile daughters; and no one would think of interfering. (Charles Darwin, *The Descent of Man* in *The Great Books of the Western World* vol. 49, ed. Robert Maynard Hutchins [Chicago: Encyclopedia Britannica, 1952], 305.

4 Chris Floyd, "A Trick of the Light: Richard Dawkins on Science and Religion," *Science & Spirit* 10/2 (July/August 1999): 26.

5 Thomas Nagel, *The Last Word* (New York: Oxford University Press, 1997), 130.

6 Richard Dawkins, *River Out of Eden: A Darwinian View of Life* (New York: Basic Books, 1995).

7 During the days of the British Raj, the average Indian was unable to differentiate between "Christendom" and many of its associations and the specific teachings of Christ himself.

8 (London: Chatto & Windus, 1946), 273.

9 *Chandogya Upanishad* 6.12-14.

10 (New York : Doubleday, 1992).

11 Arthur Peacocke, "New Wineskins for Old Wine: A Credible Theology for a Scientific World," *Science & Spirit* 10/2 (July/August 1999). Essay available on-line at http://www.science-spirit.com/articles/articledetail.cfm?article_id=78.

Chapter Two

―⚬⚬⚬―

WORLDVIEWS IN CONFLICT

Alister McGrath

The Rev. Dr. Alister McGrath is professor of theology at Oxford University. He also has a Ph.D. in molecular biophysics and is principal of Wycliffe Hall, Oxford. He is the author of 40 books, the most recent of which is A Scientific Theology I: Nature (Eerdmans).

Abstract

". . . we need to identify points of contact for the gospel . . . .
'culture-watching' can do something more than tell us about the authorities
which a culture regards as authoritative.   It reveals the fault lines within
it—namely, where a serious need, anxiety or concern exists—for example,
the threat of meaninglessness. Such points often allow us to identify ways in
which the full relevance and wonder of the Christian gospel can be effectively
and faithfully conveyed and communicated in this situation."

CHRISTIANITY OFFERS A COHERENT AND attractive worldview, which is grounded in the truth of the Christian revelation. We can see this in works as different as Augustine of Hippo's *City of God* and Abraham Kuyper's 1898 Stone Lectures at Princeton on Calvinism. Precisely because Christianity makes such major claims, we find ourselves in conflict with other worldviews, many of which are well represented on the campuses of the world's universities. Some of those worldviews are religious; there is, for example, little doubt that one of the most important struggles in which Christians are engaged in parts of Africa and Asia is with Islam, often in a highly politicized form. Others are more secular: when I was young, it was Marxism; today, it is more likely to be a form of consumerism, grounded on the basis of the belief that I am entitled to what I want.

It is important to realize that Christians have been in this situation before. One of the most important engagements in the history of the early church concerns the one with Platonism, as Christian writers sought both to communicate the truth and power of the gospel to an audience more used to thinking in Platonic ways. This involved both the identification of possibilities and threats, leading to the exploitation of those possibilities and the neutralization of those threats. The evidence at our disposal suggests that those early Christians were actually quite good at this sort of thing.

Yet Platonism went out of fashion in the early Middle Ages. Aristotle was the philosopher of choice in most Western universities from the thirteenth century until the early sixteenth century. Having mastered the contours of the dialogue with Platonism, Christian writers now had to master something significantly different. And, of course, the same process happened all over again with the rise of the "Enlightenment project," which placed such emphasis upon the competence of human reason. The evidence suggests that many evangelical theologians, especially at Princeton in the nineteenth century, developed very effective ways of handling the conflict of worldviews that resulted from the rise of rationalism in the middle of the eighteenth century.

Now we find ourselves in a new situation. Modernity is dead, we are told. Actually, this is not really true. Modernity lives on quite happily amongst Western folks who are about my age or older. But for younger people—the people on today's campuses—it is as dead as dead can be. If you are my age—I was born in 1953—or older, you live in a different cultural and intellectual world than most of those you teach. So you have a problem on your hands. Why? Because postmodernity is best understood as a deliberate rejection of the leading ideas of modernity. If we seek to commend Christianity on the basis of the modernist assumptions of the Enlightenment, we end up doing two things:

> 1. *We create a thoroughly unhealthy link between Christianity and the Enlightenment.* Remember that many of our forebears in the eighteenth century saw the Enlightenment as the enemy of faith! We've become accustomed to it since then. But that's not a good reason for defending the rationalism of the Enlightenment!

> 2. *We potentially alienate those who reject the Enlightenment, because we use its ideas and values in our defense and proclamation of the gospel.* It would be like using Platonic ideas to defend the gospel to Aristotelians—and Plato and Aristotle have a lot more in common than modernism and postmodernism!

The worldview that is arguably the most important to most Western Christian academics is that which is generally referred to as *postmodernity*. While this chapter will provide some help and guidance to anyone involved in defending and commending the Christian faith relative to any rival worldview, I have chosen to concentrate on the specific challenge posed to Christian apologetics by the rise of postmodernism. For our purposes, we could suggest that the most important feature of postmodernity is its affirmation of the individual's right to make free choices, and hence of the priority of the interpreter over what is to be interpreted. As Nietzsche once said: "There are no facts, only interpretations." If all viewpoints are thus declared equally valid, we are confronted with a worldview which encourages—even values— relativism and pluralism. This clearly raises some challenges for Christian apologists who wish to confront this important rival worldview.

Now we can handle postmodernity in several ways. We could just say that it's a good thing and overlook its many deficiencies—among which would be an aversion to matters of truth and a commitment to pluralism. Or we could say that it's a uniformly bad thing and ask that we go back to the way things were in the early twentieth century. But that's little more than nostalgia, which overlooks the *deficiencies* of postmodernism. It also fails to note that postmodernism offers important *opportunities* for the gospel, most notably in a rejection of the crude materialism or the philosophical naturalism of rationalism. The fact we must realize is that postmodernity has some aspects that we, as Christians, will cordially reject and others which we can happily live with and even commend. It's just like Platonism, Aristotelianism, and modernism: while none is specifically Christian, there will be aspects of each that we like, and others that we reject. The attitude we will have to adopt is that of *critical engagement*—that is, a principled engagement, informed and nourished by Christian principles, which allows us to critique and evaluate these rival worldviews.

Why not just reject all non-Christian worldviews? Why engage them at all? Why seek to understand and engage them? Because we want to reach those who currently adopt these worldviews build bridges to them. Initially, we must go to where they are, and subsequently we want them to cross over to where we are. Postmodernity must be *understood*— not *totally accepted*. This means trying to understand why it came into being, why some find it attractive, and where its vulnerabilities lie.

Introducing Apologetics

The area of Christian thought which deals with all aspects of this conflict of worldviews is *apologetics*.[1] Apologetics has two components: On the one hand, it concerns *the countering of objections to the Christian faith*; on the other, it concerns *setting out the attractiveness of the gospel.* It thus has both a negative and a positive aspect.

Negatively, it must encounter objections to Christianity we come across in the media and in the shopping mall. It must effectively respond to the hard questions people ask about our faith. Sometimes, those objections are spurious; sometimes they are real. But either way, these objections stand between those people and a living faith in their God and Savior. You can make a difference here by helping them see the problem is not as serious as they once thought—and even resolve it.

Positively, apologetics is about setting out the full wonder of the Christian gospel of redemption. It is like unpacking a series of wonderful gifts, and marveling at their beauty. We must help people understand the full glory of the gospel, which often means taking the trouble to explain central Christian ideas to people who may recognize the words, but not the reality they represent. Words such as *grace* and *redemption* come very easily from our lips, but we need to explain what they mean and entail to an increasingly unchurched culture. Here is the challenge: Can we effectively explain the great themes of our gospel to our unchurched friends? If we all keep thinking about the full meaning and wonder of the gospel, it will help us be more effective evangelists and deepen our own appreciation for the glory and richness of the gospel itself.

Apologetics remains of central importance to modern evangelicalism. One of the central tasks of evangelicalism is the effective and faithful proclamation of the Christian gospel. To take seriously the Great Commission to "make disciples of all nations" (Matthew 28:18-20) is to commit ourselves to all that we humanly can to ensure the gospel is preached in all its fullness and glory. It is no accident that many seminaries make "evangelism" or "mission" central themes of their teaching programs. They see these as being of essential importance to the preparation of future pastors and church leaders.

This raises the question of how evangelism and apologetics relate to each other. It is helpful to think of apologetics as a kind of pre-evangelism, something that lays the ground for evangelism at a later stage. The Greek word *apologia* literally means "a defense" or "reason for doing or believing something." The word is used with this meaning in 1 Peter 3:15, where Christians are urged to "give a reason [*apologia*] for the hope that lies within them." Apologetics is about giving reasons for faith. It is about persuading people that Christianity makes sense. Becoming a Christian does not mean throwing out our minds or kissing rational thought goodbye. Apologetics deals with barriers to faith, giving reasoned and thoughtful replies which allow our audience to appreciate fully the attraction and coherence of the Christian faith.[2]

A rough working definition of evangelism might be "inviting someone to become a Christian."[3] Apologetics would then be *clearing the ground* for that invitation so that it is more likely to receive a positive response. Evangelism is like offering someone bread. Apologetics persuades people that there is bread on offer—and that it is good to eat. Apologetics stresses the reasonableness and attractiveness of the Christian faith; evangelism makes the offer of that faith.

This all sounds rather abstract, but let's explain. Jesus often compared the gospel to a banquet or some kind of great party (e.g., Luke 14:15-24). Try to imagine two different approaches to that party. The first approach, stressing that there really is a party, explains why it is going to be great fun and reflects on the great time that everyone is going to have. The second approach issues an invitation to that party. It says: "You're invited." It asks: "Are you going to come?"

Apologetics affirms the truth and the attraction of the gospel, and evangelism issues a personal invitation to come to faith and to become a Christian. So apologetics is a kind of pre-evangelism. It prepares the way for that invitation by helping people understand what Christianity is about and why it is so attractive and meaningful. Then the way is clear for the next stage: an invitation or challenge. The analogy I have just used brings out a basic distinction between apologetics and evangelism that is too easily overlooked. Apologetics is neither confrontational nor threatening. Evangelism is confrontational—and should be! It asks someone to consider whether she feels ready to take the step of faith— a step for which apologetics has prepared the way.

But what I have just said may suggest that apologetics is just about finding good ways of getting people hooked on Christianity and neglects central themes such as the truth of the gospel. This point has been made forcefully by some evangelical writers in recent years, including Chuck Colson, Os Guinness, and David F. Wells. Let me immediately affirm that this is a serious danger. We do risk turning apologetics and evangelism into little more than effective marketing strategies, which fail to honor or recognize the truth and uniqueness of the gospel.[4] But that danger can be avoided.

One way to avoid this danger is to focus on the *theological foundation* of apologetics. Theology is essential to good apologetics in two manners. First, *it provides the apologist with a network of beliefs and doctrines, to enable him to detect weaknesses in alternative worldviews and to identify the strengths of the Christian proclamation.* For example, the apologetics by Francis Schaeffer argued that, for theological reasons, every non-Christian worldview would collapse under the pressure of internal contradictions when its implications are pressed to their limit. We must be convinced that the Christian gospel is true—even in a postmodern culture that regards truth as unimportant.

Theology is important in a second way. *It provides the apologist with a way to bring the full resources of the Christian gospel to bear on the situation.* Theological analysis allows the complex unity of the Christian faith to be broken down into its constituent parts so that the apologist can decide which of its many aspects can best be used in a particular situation. The enormously rich Christian proclamation of the death and resurrection of Christ can thus be analyzed, in order that its various aspects can be identified and exploited.

Learning from the Acts of the Apostles

In a pluralist world, where the good news is proclaimed amongst many faiths and worldviews, we should remind ourselves that we have been here before. My Oxford colleague Michael Green has pointed out these similarities and their importance to our situation:

> I find it ironic that people object to the proclamation of the Christian gospel these days because so many other faiths jostle on the doorstep of our global village. What's new? The variety of faiths in antiquity was even greater than it is today. And the early Christians, making as they did ultimate claims for Jesus, met the problem of other faiths head-on from the very outset. Their approach was interesting . . . They did not denounce other faiths. They simply proclaimed Jesus with all the power and persuasiveness at their disposal.[5]

It is my firm belief that we can learn from these early apologetic approaches to the manner in which we proclaim Jesus to modern Western culture. They offer us insights into authentically biblical methods of apologetics, as well as strategies for engaging with specific groups which were of major importance to the development of the early church. My approach will explore the broad apologetic strategies developed by Paul in a key speech in Acts.

One of the most important audiences for the gospel proclamation were "the Greeks." In Paul's first letter to the Corinthians, "the Greeks" are set alongside "the Jews" as a defining group of considerable importance (1 Corinthians 1:22). The book of Acts clearly exhibits at least some degree of familiarity and affinity with Hellenistic rhetoric[6] as well as the beliefs and practices of classical paganism. Paul preaches the gospel in a pluralist culture, in which worldviews jostled for influence, and there was no overarching worldview. It is a world that resembles our postmodern situation.

What can be learned from how the gospel is presented in such situations? One of the most important descriptions of the early confrontation between Christianity and classical paganism is found in Paul's Areopagus address at Athens. Paul opens this address with a gradual introduction of the theme of the living God. Notice how he lays the foundation for this theme. He does not presuppose familiarity with the idea of the one, true and living God of Israel. When Paul or Peter addressed Jewish audiences, this concept could be taken for granted; the purpose of the address was to show how Jesus of Nazareth radically altered matters and how faith in Jesus was necessary for a relationship with the living God they had described.

However, here—as in Paul's address to the people of Lystra (Acts 14:15-17)—no such pre-understanding can be assumed. The basic theme of a living, personal God needed to be introduced before the fundamental themes of the gospel can be enunciated. This simple observation is of considerable apologetic importance.

Some of the people to whom we wish to preach the gospel have only the most rudimentary understanding of Christianity. Everything needs to be introduced and explained. We can assume very little knowledge of Christian ideas, words, and meanings on the part of many of those with whom we speak. Paul, knowing Greek pagan religion had relatively little to say concerning a living personal God, introduces and explains the idea. We need to learn from that. We need to introduce and explain terms!

Second, notice also how Paul appeals to a pagan poet. Acts 17:27-28 cites two pagan poets, one of whom has not been identified with total certainty, the other of which is Aratus. Aratus' *Phenomena* would have been known and appreciated by his audience. In making his points, Paul cites authorities who are familiar and valued by his audience.

Third, notice that Paul builds on their existing understanding of things. In other words, he identifies aspects of their beliefs that can act as "points of contact" for the gospel. This sermon may be seen as an illustration of Paul's desire to "be all things to all people" in action. He deliberately identifies aspects of the gospel that are most likely to find sympathy with his audience with a view to building on these subsequently. Paul declares that the Athenians are noted for their religiosity; he therefore builds on this interest. The religious and philosophical curiosity of the Athenians shaped the contours of his theological exposition.[7] The "sense of divinity" present in each individual is here used as a powerful apologetic device, by which Paul is able to base his message upon acceptable Greek theistic assumptions, while at the same time going beyond them. Paul shows a clear appreciation of the apologetic potential of Stoic philosophy, portraying the gospel as resonating with central Stoic concerns, while extending the limits of what might be known. What the Greeks held to be unknown, possibly unknowable, Paul proclaims to have been made known through the resurrection of Christ. The entire episode illustrates the manner in which Paul is able to take advantage of the situation and persuade his audience—without compromising the integrity of faith.

At this point, we need to consider the inscription on the altar to which Paul refers: "to an unknown god" (Acts 17:23). There are certainly classical precedents for this, especially according to the writings of Diogenes Laertius. Numerous Christian writers of the early patristic period explained Paul's meaning by appealing to the "anonymous altars" which were scattered throughout the region at that time. Several (including Didymus of Alexandria) suggested that Paul may have altered the inscription from the plural ("to unknown gods"). However, there is no reason to suppose that Paul made any such change.

The fundamental point is that a deity of whom the Greeks had some implicit or intuitive awareness is being made known to them by name and in full. The god who is known indirectly through his creation can be known fully in redemption. Notice how Paul explicitly appeals to the idea of creation as a basis for his apologetic approach. Paul here seems to use the theme of creation as a *praeparatio evangelica*, a way of introducing the theme of redemption in Christ. Paul believed passionately in the theological truth and apologetic importance of this insight (Romans 1- 2). If Paul is right, it should not surprise us that we can discern "signals of transcendence" (in Peter Berger's words) within human life.[8] If there is some point of contact already in existence, then apologetics does not need to establish the foundations of the Christian knowledge of God; it can make use of a God-given starting point, within the very nature of the created order itself. The witness to God in creation acts as a trigger, stimulating people to ask about the meaning of life or the reality of God. Those points of contact are already there, given within the created order. The apologist must identify and exploit them. They are meant to be there—and they are meant to be used.

A point of contact is thus a God-given foothold for divine self-revelation. It is a catalyst, not a substitute, for God's self-revelation. It is like the advance guard of an army, preparing the ground for the major force that follows it. It is like the pre-strike of a bolt of lightning, in which a conductive path is established from earth to the sky so that the massive energy of the lightning can discharge itself fully into the waiting earth. When God gives himself in the act of revelation; there is, however, a sense in which he has prepared the ground for that giving— not to pre-empt it, nor to make it unnecessary, but simply to make it more effective when it happens.

How can we use this approach apologetically today? It is an enormously rich approach. In what follows, we shall explore ways of drawing on it in our modern situation. I shall focus on ways in which Christian academics can exploit some important opportunities. Since my own background is in the natural sciences, I hope you will forgive me for focusing on these.

The biblical writers are aware of the majesty and wonder of God being revealed through nature. "The heavens declare the glory of God; the skies proclaim the work of his hands" (Psalm 19:1). The doctrine of creation gives theological foundation to the notion of a natural knowledge of God. If God created the world, it is to be expected that his creation should bear the mark of God's special handiwork. Just as an artist's distinctive style might be evident in her sculpting, or a painter might sign his name on his work, so the presence of God can be discerned within the creation.

The fact that the human mind can discern and investigate this ordering of nature is significant. There is something about human nature that prompts it to ask questions about the world. And there seems to be something about the world that allows answers to those questions to be given. The noted theoretical physicist and Christian apologist John Polkinghorne comments on this in his *Science and Creation*:

> We are so familiar with the fact that we can understand the world that most of the time we take it for granted. It is what makes science possible. Yet it could have been otherwise. The universe might have been a disorderly choas rather than an orderly cosmos. Or it might have had a rationality which was inaccessible to us. . . . There is a congruence between our minds and the universe, between the rationality experienced within and the rationality observed without.[9]

There is a deep-seated congruence between the rationality present in our minds and the rationality—the orderedness—that we observe as present in the world. Thus the abstract structures of pure mathematics provide important clues to understanding the world. All of this, Polkinghorne argues, is a form of natural theology, preparing the way for the full knowledge of the Christian revelation.

Nevertheless, Polkinghorne is clear that more is needed than this awareness of the explicability of the world. Having devoted several chapters of one of his books to a survey of some points of contact for the gospel, he notes:

> The kinds of consideration outlined in the preceding chapters would, I think, incline me to take a theistic view of the world. By themselves that is about as far as

they would get me. The reason why I take my stand within the Christian community lies in certain events which took place in Palestine nearly two thousand years ago.[10]

In other words, the life, death and resurrection of Jesus of Nazareth are critical in confirming what the creation hints at. (Note here how Paul, having spoken of the importance of creation, clinches his argument by an appeal to the resurrection in Acts 17:31.) Points of contact—such as that identified here by Polkinghorne—can help create receptivity towards theism, including Christianity.

Theologians have developed natural theologies, based on the sense of beauty that arises from contemplating the world. Hans Urs von Balthasar is an example of a twentieth-century writer who stresses the theological importance of beauty. But perhaps the most powerful exploration of this theme is due to the celebrated American theologian, Jonathan Edwards. In his *Personal Narrative*, Edwards wrote thus of his "sheer beholding of God's beauty":

> As I was walking there and looking up into the sky and clouds, there came into my mind so sweet a sense of the glorious *majesty* and *grace* of God, that I know not how to express. I seemed to see them both in a sweet conjunction . . . it was a sweet and gentle, and holy majesty; and also a majestic meekness.[11]

This sense of aesthetic ecstasy pervades Edwards' autobiographical writings, especially his *Miscellanies*. The perception of beauty that we experience "when we are delighted with flowery meadows and gentle breezes" is, for Edwards, an intimation of the holiness of God, which Scripture clarifies and confirms, placing it upon a reliable theological foundation.

These, then, are merely some of the ways in which Christian theologians have attempted to describe the manner in which God can be known through nature. In each case, a variant of the apostle Paul's approach is used. The Creator can be known! The 'unknown' God has chosen to make himself known! These are the great discernible themes in Paul's sermon to the Areopagites.

45

Apologetic Strategies

On our campuses, one of the issues we face in the conflict of worldviews is the need for seasoned role models. In this section I want to look at two significant apologists of the twentieth century and ask what we might learn from them. Both people I have chosen exercised a significant academic ministry—one as a leading representative of one of the world's greatest universities and the other as an independent operator, who chose to engage the academic world of his day from his mountain retreat in Switzerland. Each of them has important insights to offer us.

C. S. Lewis

C.S. Lewis is an important resource for Christian academics. Not only is he an authority on English literature, especially Milton, but he was also an important writer. His writings continue to be read and appreciated. Lewis was aware of certain deep human emotions which pointed to a dimension of our existence beyond time and space. There is, Lewis suggested, a deep and intense feeling of longing within human beings, which no earthly object or experience can satisfy. Lewis terms this sense "joy" and argues that it points to God as its source and goal (hence the title of his autobiography, *Surprised by Joy*). Joy, according to Lewis, is "an unsatisfied desire which is itself more desirable than any other satisfaction . . . anyone who has experienced it will want it again."[12]

Lewis explored this matter further in a remarkable sermon entitled "The Weight of Glory," preached before the University of Oxford on 8 June 1941. Lewis spoke of "a desire which no natural happiness will satisfy," "a desire, still wandering and uncertain of its object and still largely unable to see that object in the direction where it really lies." There is something self-defeating about human desire, in that what is desired, when achieved, seems to leave the desire unsatisfied. Lewis illustrates this from the age-old quest for beauty, using recognizably Augustinian imagery:

> The books or the music in which we thought the beauty
> was located will betray us if we trust to them; it was not
> in them, it only came through them, and what came

through them was longing. These things—the beauty, the memory of our own past—are good images of what we really desire; but if they are mistaken for the thing itself they turn into dumb idols, breaking the hearts of their worshippers. For they are not the thing itself; they are only the scent of a flower we have not found, the echo of a tune we have not heard, news from a country we have not visited.[13]

Human desire, the deep and bitter-sweet longing for something that will satisfy us, points beyond finite objects and finite persons (who seem able to fulfill this desire, yet eventually prove incapable of doing so); it points *through* these objects and persons towards their real goal and fulfillment in God himself. It is as if human love points to something beyond it, as with a parable.

The paradox of hedonism—the simple, yet stultifying, fact that pleasure cannot satisfy—is another instance of this curious phenomenon. Even in our contentment, we still feel the need of something which is indefinably missing, but whose absence seems only too real. It is as if God leaves us with a certain weariness with nature, which can only be satisfied by pressing on beyond nature to its source and goal in God himself. George Herbert's poem *The Pulley* is a splendid meditation on this sense of weariness with the world, which drives some to seek (and find) God. Herbert reflects on how a man might find all the riches in nature, and yet remain discontent—and by experiencing this dissatisfaction, come to find God:

> Let him keep the rest,
> But keep them with repining restlessness.
> Let him be rich and weary, that at last,
> If goodness lead him not, yet weariness
> May toss him to my breast.

If meditation on the goodness of God does not drive us to him, perhaps weariness with the pleasures of the world will have the intended effect.

Pleasure, beauty, personal relationships—all seem to promise so much, and yet when we grasp them, we find that what we were seeking was not located in them. It lies beyond them. There is a "divine dissatisfaction" within human experience, which prompts us to ask, "Will anything satisfy the human quest to fulfill the desires of the human heart?"

Lewis argues that there is. Hunger, he suggests, is an excellent example of a human sensation that corresponds to a real physical need. This need points to the existence of food by which it may be met. Thirst, according to Lewis, is a further example of a human longing pointing to a human need, which in turn points to its fulfillment in drinking—if the human being in question is to survive. Any human longing, he argues, points to a genuine human need, which in turn points to a real object corresponding to that need. And so, Lewis suggests, the deep human sense of infinite longing which cannot be satisfied by any physical or finite object or person must point to a real human need which can, in some way, be met. Lewis argues that this sense of longing points to its origin and its fulfillment in God himself.

An English literature class or lecture series could thus become an exploration of how this theme of "joy" (to use Lewis' term) is expressed, and what its significance might be. This is an important apologetic device. *A worldview must be able to account for this experience of an unsatisfied longing—and that the gospel has precisely this capacity.* It does not merely explain the origins of this sense of dissatisfaction; it must also have the power to satisfy us. Making this point is important in this conflict of worldviews!

Francis Schaeffer

All worldviews, all belief systems rest upon presuppositions. Francis Schaeffer develops this point as follows in *The God Who is There.*

> Let us remember that every person we speak to . . . has a set of presuppositions, whether he or she has analyzed them or not . . . It is impossible for any non-Christian individual or group to be consistent to their system in logic or in practice . . . A man may try to bury the tension and you may have to help him find it, but somewhere there is a point of inconsistency. He stands

in a position which he cannot pursue to the end; and this is not just an intellectual concept of tension, it is what is wrapped up in what he is as a man.[14]

The basic point Schaeffer makes is of considerable importance to a person-centered apologetic. You can tease out the presuppositions upon which their lives rest. It is quite possible that their lives are actually grounded on a whole set of unrecognized presuppositions, which your gentle and patient inquiry can bring to light. Experience suggests that such gentle explorations can sometimes be devastating, in that they expose the inner contradictions and confusions within someone's outlook on life. A crisis may result, in which faith can be born.

Schaeffer provides a number of examples of cases in which exposure of contradictions and tensions within worldviews has important (and negative) implications for their credibility. I will note two. The first is illustrated by a discussion group Schaeffer was leading at Cambridge University, attended by a young Sikh:

> He started to speak strongly against Christianity, but did not really understand the problems of his own beliefs. So I said, "Am I not correct in saying that on the basis of your system, cruelty and noncruelty are ultimately equal, that there is no intrinsic difference between them?" He agreed. . . . The student in whose room we met, who had clearly understood the implications of what the Sikh had admitted, picked up his kettle of boiling water with which he was about to make tea, and stood with it steaming over the Indian's head. The man looked up and asked him what he was doing, and he said with a cold yet gentle finality, "There is no difference between cruelty and noncruelty." Thereupon the [Indian] walked out into the night.[15]

The point Schaeffer makes here is that persistent questioning exposed the inner contradiction within an alternative belief system. The same point is illustrated in a more celebrated example, where Schaeffer skillfully deploys it against the ethical nihilism of Jean-Paul Sartre.

Sartre's fundamental point was that ethics is irrelevant. Any ethical component of an action lies in the exercise of choice, not the moral decision reached. This famous attitude attracted considerable attention. When Sartre signed the Algerian Manifesto—a protest against the continuing French occupation of Algeria, events in the real world called into question his ethical views:

> [Sartre] took up a deliberately moral attitude and said it was an unjust and dirty war. His left-wing political position which he took up is another illustration of the same inconsistency. As far as many secular existentialists have been concerned, from the moment Sartre signed the Algerian Manifesto he was regarded as an apostate from his own position, and toppled from his place of leadership of the avant-garde.[16]

Schaeffer's point was that Sartre and other nihilists "could not live with the conclusions of their system." So apologists need to explore what those conclusions might be. "The more logical a man who holds a non-Christian position is to his own presuppositions, the further he is from the real world; and the nearer he is to the real world, the more illogical he is to his own presuppositions."[17]

Schaeffer develops this insight further by analyzing the way in which worldviews construct shields to protect themselves against the real world. The apologist must remove that shield, and allow the harsh realities of the real world to raise questions about the credibility of that system:

> It is like the great shelters built upon some mountain passes to protect vehicles from the avalanches of rock and stone which periodically tumble down the mountain. The avalanche, in the case of the non-Christian, is the real and the abnormal fallen world which surrounds him. The Christian, lovingly, must remove the shelter and allow the truth of the external world and of what man is to beat upon him.[18]

Just as Sartre's views proved untenable when confronted with the crises and situations of the real world, so other worldviews, according to Schaeffer, can be discredited in similar ways. Discovering the implications of outlooks is of major apologetic importance, as is a willingness to explore them, gently and lovingly, with those who cling fast to them.

As an academic, you can encourage your students to challenge some of the wisdom of our age, which passes as knowledge. Our culture is prone to accept all worldviews as equally good. Like Schaeffer, you can challenge that assumption to help them to see that truth matters.

Earlier, I pointed out that apologetics has both positive and negative aspects. It involves *identifying* problems and *responding* to them, on the one hand. On the other hand, it involves *articulating* the full wonder and joy of the gospel in terms that the culture can understand. Addressing a postmodern audience forces us to look at both these matters. Postmodernity raises specific and serious challenges to the gospel, particularly in relation to truth. "It may be true for you, but that doesn't mean it's true for me" is a depressingly common response to evangelism and reflects the basic ethos of postmodernity.

It is also painfully clear that postmodernity has no notion of sin and no belief in hell. Anyone attempting to convert a postmodern person on the basis of a preexisting belief in either of these is in for a rough time. We do not need to persuade someone of sin or hell before we proclaim the gospel. As John and Charles Wesley demonstrate—to note only one or two of many examples that could be given—preaching the love of God can be gateway to the recognition of our sin and need for redemption. We must avoid becoming trapped in the habits of thought characteristic of, for example, classic nineteenth-century evangelical gospel preaching, which was developed with the assumptions of Victorian culture (which focused on sin and hell!).[19]

Conclusion

In this chapter, I cannot hope to give a full defense of the Christian claim to be telling the truth against postmodern skepticism. There is neither time nor space.[20] But I should stress the importance of identifying firsthand the specifics of a culture through listening and watching. My experience as an apologist has led me to conclude that a *good apologist listens and watches before speaking.*

And what of opportunities? Paul appealed to an "unknown God" at Athens; Peter appealed to the trajectory of salvation history, which culminated in Christ. To what do we make our appeal? There are a number of postmodern issues that offer natural and important ways to preach the gospel with vigor and rigor. For example, in a garden in which a thousand flowers bloom, a lot of them turn out to be poisonous weeds. The quest for relevance, meaning, and love is always there, and we need to identify and address it. For me, one of the most wonderful things about the Christian gospel is that we do not need to make it attractive. Like a pearl of great price, it already *is* attractive. Our task as apologists is to allow that attractiveness to be seen, articulated and appreciated.

My fundamental point is that we must try to understand our audience and the particular constraints this places upon us. I suspect the evangelist who preaches the same sermon in each and every evangelistic context does not really engage with the issues. He must ensure that the richness of the Christian proclamation is firmly and properly located with reference to the audience being addressed.

For example, we should adopt a different apologetic approach when addressing Oxford University students who are specializing in the study of quantum electrodynamics than we do speaking to an audience of Jewish rabbis. The identity of that audience is going to have a major impact on three matters: (1) the *terminology* we use, (2) the *authorities* to which we appeal, and (3) the *points of contact* which we discern for the gospel.

First, let's look at the *terminology* we use. Words familiar to us—such as *grace* and *redemption*—require explanation to an increasingly unchurched culture. C. S. Lewis, unquestionably the greatest apologist of his time,[21] made this point memorably:

> We must learn the language of our audience. And let me say at the outset that it is no use laying down a priori what the 'plain man' does or does not understand. You have to find out by experience . . . You must translate every bit of your theology into the vernacular. This is

> very troublesome . . . but it is essential. It is also of the
> greatest service to your own thought. I have come to
> the conclusion that if you cannot translate your own
> thoughts into uneducated language, then your
> thoughts are confused. Power to translate is the test of
> having really understood your own meaning.[22]

We must also use *authorities* that relate to the audience: Sometimes we appeal to Scripture, but forget that those we are addressing do not attribute any authority to Scripture. The Apostle Paul, speaking to a Greek audience which was clearly unfamiliar with the Old Testament, was not in the least discouraged. He simply adopted a different approach—one which built upon what Paul Ricoeur call "the available believable." Modern Western culture is increasingly biblically illiterate. Paul reminds us that we do not need to persuade people of the authority of Scripture before we proclaim the gospel! Recognition of scriptural authority comes after a recognition of the authority of the risen Christ as Savior and Lord.

So what authorities does postmodernity regard as carrying weight? Here, we need to note the importance of culture-watching—that is, observing our culture and its potential audiences, to note what figures, texts, and values it regards as possessing authority. To gain a hearing we may need to appeal to those authorities in much the same way Paul appealed to the Greek poet at Athens. We need to study the patterns of reasoning and argument which carry weight for a given audience—just as Paul used classic Roman forensic rhetoric to defend himself and the gospel in the Roman courts.

This may be difficult for some of us. I know next to nothing about Nirvana, Oasis or many postmodern icons. In fact, by the time I have come to understand them, they will probably be out of date. I would be a lousy apologist to such audiences—but, by the grace of God, there are others who can make those connections and relate to those particular audiences. It seems to me that there is a real need for specialist apologetic ministries, reflecting an *incarnational principle*: that is, that you embed yourself in the culture which you are seeking to saturate with the good news of Christ.

Yet it is important to note that a postmodern audience is not monolithic. There are some today who still know something about the Bible. For example, some might respond to an "Acts 2" rather than an "Acts 17" approach. We need to understand that audience before making that judgment. While much of postmodernity rejects the notion of "absolute truth," this is not universal. We may well find that the tried and tested approaches of apologists dating from the heydey of modernism still work in some quarters, even if their assumptions would be rejected outright in many others.

Finally, we need to identify *points of contact* for the gospel. Let us recall at this point that 'culture-watching' can do something more than tell us about the authorities which a culture regards as authoritative. It reveals the *fault lines* within it—namely, where a serious need, anxiety or concern exists—for example, the threat of meaninglessness. Such points often allow us to identify ways in which the full relevance and wonder of the Christian gospel can be effectively and faithfully conveyed and communicated in this situation.

I have offered what I am aware is a painfully superficial engagement with a series of vast issues. However, I believe it is worth taking this risk in order to identify and open the way to further exploration of some approaches that I believe are profoundly worthwhile and important. The Acts of the Apostles invites us to rediscover biblical approaches to apologetics and to make the task of the apostles our own. I trust and pray we may learn from the example of those earliest Christians as we prepare to enter the third millennium of the new covenant.

Many Christian academics long to serve God more effectively and see their role as scholars as offering important strategic opportunities for service. My purpose here is to affirm this belief and offer thoughts on how evangelical scholars can begin more effectively to develop their ministries.

There is much justified anxiety about the secularism, relativism and pluralism which is endemic in much of today's American higher education. Evangelicals and many others as well—have noted with growing concern that the modern American academy seems to have more to do with elitism, ideological warfare, and rampant anti-religious propaganda than with learning. Yet, Christian academics must be there as salt and light. Why?

The story is told of a conversation between two of the most celebrated German liberal Protestant theologians of the nineteenth century, Albrecht Ritschl and Adolf Harnack. The more conservative sections of the German Protestant churches had recently gained some significant political victories. Ritschl's advice to Harnack is reported to be: "Never mind about the politics—get on with writing the books that will change the way people think. In the long term, that is what will be of decisive importance." The sustained gains made by liberal German Protestantism up to the eve of the first World War, demonstrate the wisdom of Ritschl's advice. To win long-term victories, you must influence the way a rising generation thinks.

How can evangelical scholars serve God within the academy—whether working in biology, history, theology, or physics? First, we need a *vision*. We need to realize that each of us can make a difference. Through God's good grace, we can help people capture a sense of the wonder and glory of the Christian gospel. Sometimes it will be through the things we say. At other times, it will be through the things we do. In his providence, God has placed us somewhere special—somewhere that he can use us. We all need to start asking questions like: "Why has God placed me here?"

The basic issue is building a vision—a vision of who God is and the way in which he can use us. We need to catch a fresh vision of the glory of God and the wonderful fact that God takes pleasure in using weak and foolish people such as ourselves to further his purposes and advance his kingdom. One thing Paul learned through the "thorn in the flesh" incident was that the grace of God was sufficient for him and that God's strength was made perfect in weakness. Believing we can make a difference to people is not about being arrogant; it is about trusting in the grace and promises of God.

Second, we need to *ask what special opportunities are open to us through the subject which we teach*. For example, the physicist can point to the remarkable order of the universe as pointing to the wisdom of God as its Creator. John Calvin suggested that astronomers and medical physicians are in an especially privileged position because they are able to see the invisible God embodied in creation. A professor of Christian literature would be in a position to introduce students to the writings of Dorothy L. Sayers, G. K. Chesterton, and C. S. Lewis—important works in their own right, yet possessing special importance through their ability to express some of the central themes of Christianity.

The need to identify apologetic possibilities in our areas of teaching or research leads naturally to my third point—*the importance of fellowship with other evangelical scholars*. It is easy to become lonely and discouraged as an evangelical scholar. It helps to meet up with others and find comfort in their company. We can pray together or exchange ideas. What approaches have worked for us? It is important to share wisdom and insights that have been won at great expense. One reason I believe this *God and the Academy* conference to be so important is the opportunities it will bring for networking, dialogue, prayer and fellowship.

Fourthly, we need to *identify role models*—that is, scholars who have managed to bring together faith and learning in their own professional careers and whose wisdom and example can inspire others. By this, I do not mean that we blindly and woodenly imitate them! Rather, role models should be seen as an encouragement and inspiration. We have lost sight of some of the great themes in evangelical history. What we now call "mentoring" was seen as being of immense importance. Yet this is something we can recover. Those who have given much thought to bringing together faith and scholarship have both the privilege and responsibility of helping those at an earlier stage in their careers who are seeking to do the same.

How do we identify role models, and how do we ensure there will be role models in the future? Based on my observation of the situation in the United Kingdom, such figures of excellence seem to have just happened. In other words, there was no conscious attempt by others to encourage them to develop such a role; it was something that just developed as things went along.

We need to be more proactive here. We need to identify future role models early and encourage them to deliberately and purposefully plan for this possibility, prayerfully and in consultation with colleagues. Their future role could be immensely important. So we need to give thought to this now.

Finally, *we need to be aware that evangelical scholars come in two different categories—the teachers and the researchers*. Each has their own distinct gifts and merits, and both must be honored and encouraged. Many owe the consolidation of their faith and the beginnings of their attempts to relate faith and learning to the patient teaching and personal example of those who first taught them and introduced them to the great themes which would shape their future careers. Great researchers can stimulate the process of reflection and consolidation that turns someone on fire with excitement about God and his or her discipline. But the foundation needs to be there first.

Saint Paul used the analogy of the human body to explain that every member of the body of Christ has a role to play. We must not allow ourselves to value one member more than another when *all* are required for the healthy functioning of the body. Whether we are committed to teaching or research at the cutting edge of our field, we must keep this broader perspective in mind. We all need each other. Together, we can do things for God which we could not possibly manage on our own. And we need to be reminded of our total dependence upon the grace of God—in case we begin to get big ideas about our own importance!

A great challenge lies ahead. How can we bring our faith to the life of the academy? How can God continue to be found at Harvard? At Oxford? At wherever we have the privilege of teaching or researching? Some immensely challenging and exciting times lie ahead. We need to prepare for them. I hope and trust we will all come away from the conference with a vision to give us a new sense of purpose and perspective on our lives as scholars and teachers.

---

[1] For a more detailed exploration of this distinction, see Alister E. McGrath, *Intellectuals Don't Need God and Other Modern Myths* (Grand Rapids: Zondervan, 1994).

[2] For some of the approaches available, see T. R. Phillips and D. L. Okholm, *Christian Apologetics in the Postmodern World* (Downers Grove, Ill.: InterVarsity Press, 1995).

[3] I set to one side here the important discussion of the relation of the human and the divine in evangelism—a theme which merits a full analysis in its own right.

[4] An excellent example may be found in David F. Wells, *No Place for Truth; or, Whatever Happened to Evangelical Theology?* (Grand Rapids.: Eerdmans, 1993), which documents the rise of pragmatic and "therapeutic" concerns within evangelicalism—often at the expense of a concern for truth.

[5] Michael Green, *Acts for Today: First-Century Christianity for Twentieth-Century Christians* (London: Hodder & Stoughton, 1993), 38.

[6] See W. S. Kurz, "Hellenistic Rhetoric in the Christological Proofs of Luke-Acts," *Catholic Biblical Quarterly* 42 (1980): 171—95.

[7] See Bertil Gartner, *The Areopagus Speech and Natural Revelation* (Uppsala: Gleerup, 1955).

[8] See Peter Berger, *A Rumor of Angels*, 2nd ed. (New York: Doubleday, 1990).

[9] John Polkinghorne, *Science and Creation: The Search for Understanding* (London: SPCK, 1988), 20-1.

[10] John Polkinghorne, *The Way the World Is* (London: SPCK, 1983), 33.

[11] Cited by Robert W. Jenson, *America's Theologian: A Recommendation of Jonathan Edwards* (New York: Oxford University Press, 1988), 19.

[12] C. S. Lewis, *Surprised by Joy* (London: Collins, 1959), 20.

[13] C. S. Lewis, *Screwtape Proposes A Toast* (London: Collins, 1965), 97-8.

[14] Francis Schaeffer, *Trilogy* (Leicester: InterVarsity Press, 1990), 132-3.

[15] Ibid., 110.

[16] Ibid., 58.

[17] Ibid., 134.

[18] Ibid., 140.

[19] Interested readers might like to dip into Geoffrey Rowell's fascinating study *Hell and the Victorians* (Oxford: Clarendon Press, 1974).

[20] But I could refer you to a substantial discussion of the issue in Alister E. McGrath, *A Passion for Truth: The Intellectual Coherence of Evangelicalism* (Leicester: InterVarsity Press, 1994), 163-200.

[21] See the assessment provided by Basil Mitchell, "Contemporary Challenges to Christian Apologetics," in *How to Play Theological Ping-Pong* (London: Hodder & Stoughton, 1990), 25-41 (esp. 25).

[22] C. S. Lewis, *God in the Dock* (Grand Rapids: Eerdmans, 1970), 96.

Chapter Three

—⌇⌇—

ACADEMIC INTEGRATION
AND THE CHRISTIAN SCHOLAR

J. P. Moreland

Dr. J.P. Moreland is professor of philosophy at Talbot School of Theology in La Mirada, California. He has written books such as Christianity and the Nature of Science (Baker), Scaling the Secular City (Baker), and Love Your God With All Your Mind (Navpress). He has contributed to many professional journals, writing extensively in the area of metaphysics and the philosophy of science.

Abstract

"Because Christians are interested in the truth for its own sake and because they are called to proclaim and defend their views to an unbelieving world and to seek to live consistently with those views, it is important for members of the believing community to think carefully about how to integrate their carefully formed theological beliefs with prominent claims in other fields of study."

THOUGHTFUL CHRISTIANS ARE AGREED that an important component of Christian scholarship is the integration of faith and learning, as it is sometimes called. Because Christians are interested in the truth for its own sake and because they are called to proclaim and defend their views to an unbelieving world and to seek to live consistently with those views, it is important for members of the believing community to think carefully about how to integrate their carefully formed theological beliefs with prominent claims in other fields of study. As St. Augustine wisely asserted, "We must show our Scriptures not to be in conflict with whatever [our critics] can demonstrate about the nature of things from reliable sources."[1] However, the task of integration is hard work, and there is no widespread agreement about how it is to be done generally or about what its results should look like in specific cases. In what follows, I shall do three things to contribute to the integrative enterprise: 1) describe the relation between integration and spiritual formation; 2) discuss current integrative priorities for the Christian scholar; 3) analyze the epistemic tasks for and models employed in integration.

Integration as an Expression of and Aid to Spiritual Formation

Before we proceed, it is crucial that we reflect a bit further on what is so important about the task of integration at this particular moment in the church's history. To begin with, there is a widespread hunger throughout our culture for genuine, life-transforming spirituality. This is as it should be. People are weary of those who claim to believe certain things when they do not see those beliefs having an impact on the lives of the heralds. Among other things, integration is a spiritual activity We may even call it a spiritual discipline, but not merely in the sense that often comes to mind in this context. Often, Christian scholars express the spiritual aspect of integration in terms of *doxology*. The Christian integrator holds to and teaches the same beliefs about her subject matter that non-Christians accept but goes on to add praise to God for the subject matter. Thus, the Christian biologist simply asserts the views widely accepted in the discipline but makes sure that class closes with a word of praise to God for the beauty and complexity of the living world.

The doxological approach is good as far as it goes; unfortunately, it does not go far enough in capturing the spiritual dimension of integration. We draw closer to the core of this dimension when we think about the role of beliefs in the process of spiritual transformation. Beliefs are the rails upon which our lives run. We almost always act according to what we really believe. It does not matter much what we say we believe or what we want others to think we believe. When the rubber meets the road, we act out our actual beliefs most of the time. That is why behavior is such a good indicator of a person's beliefs. The centrality of beliefs for spiritual progress is a clear implication of Old Testament teaching on wisdom and New Testament teaching about the role of a renewed mind in transformation. Thus, integration has as its spiritual aim the intellectual goal of *structuring* the mind so a person can see things as they really are and *strengthening* the belief structure that ought to inform the individual and corporate life of discipleship unto Jesus. Integration can aid a believer in maintaining and developing convictions about those beliefs

Integration can also help an unbeliever to accept certain beliefs crucial to the Christian journey. This aspect of integration becomes clear when we reflect on the notion of a plausibility structure. A person will never be able to change his life if he cannot even entertain the beliefs needed to bring about that change. By "entertain a belief" I mean to consider the *possibility* that the belief *might* be true. A person's *plausibility structure* is the set of ideas the person either is or is not willing to entertain as possibly true. For example, no one would come to a lecture defending a flat earth because this idea is just not part of our plausibility structure. We cannot even entertain the idea. Moreover, a person's plausibility structure is largely (though not exclusively) a function of the beliefs he already has. Applied to accepting or maintaining Christian belief, J. Gresham Machen got it right when he said,

> [God] usually exerts that power in connection with certain prior conditions of the human mind, and it should be ours to create, so far as we can, with the help of God, those favorable conditions for the reception of

the gospel. False ideas are the greatest obstacles to the reception of the gospel. We may preach with all the fervor of a reformer and yet succeed only in winning a straggler here and there, if we permit the whole collective thought of the nation or of the world to be controlled by ideas which, by the resistless force of logic, prevent Christianity from being regarded as anything more than a harmless delusion.[2]

If a culture reaches the point where Christian claims are not even part of its plausibility structure, fewer and fewer people will be able to entertain the possibility that they might be true. Whatever stragglers do come to faith in such a context would do so on the basis of felt needs alone and the genuineness of such conversions would be questionable to say the least. And believers will not make much progress in the spiritual life because they will not have the depth of conviction or the integrated noetic (knowledge) structure necessary for such progress. This is why integration is so crucial to spirituality. It can create a plausibility structure in a person's mind—favorable conditions as Machen put it—so Christian ideas can be entertained by that person.

Current Integrative Priorities for the Christian Scholar

But how does a Christian scholar decide on what to spend her energies in the integrative task? There are so many areas of study. What criteria are there to help one prioritize her efforts? Is there a taxonomy of issues that expresses some priorities that Christian scholars ought to adopt? I'm afraid I have a lot more thinking to do on this before I am prepared to offer anything approximating an adequate answer to these questions. Any taxonomy here would likely express the interests and biases of the taxonomist, and I am no exception to this rule. Obviously, one's own sense of personal calling and one's own curiosities will and should play an important role here.

However, I think the following three criteria are not too wide of the mark. First, integration should be focused on those *areas of study that seem to be intrinsically more central or foundational to the Christian theistic enterprise.* The deeply ingrained metaphysical, epistemological, and axiological commitments that constitute mere Christianity should be preserved. Second, integration should be focused on *areas that are currently under heavy attack.* A third and, perhaps, less important criterion is this: integration should be focused on those *areas of study in which such activity is under-represented, relatively speaking.*

It is the task of Christian scholars in each discipline to decide how these criteria inform their intellectual work. However, I think points one and two converge so as to yield an integrative mandate for contemporary Christian scholars, especially those who work on the interface between science and Christian faith. A very important cultural fact that Christian scholars must face when they undertake the task of integration is this: *There simply is no established, widely recognized body of ethical or religious knowledge now operative in the institutions of knowledge in our culture,* e.g., the universities. Indeed, ethical and religious claims are frequently placed into what Francis Schaeffer used to call the "upper story." They are judged to have little or no epistemic authority, especially compared to the authority given to science to define the limits of knowledge and reality in those same institutions. This raises a pressing question: Is Christianity a knowledge tradition or merely a faith traditional perspective which, while true, cannot be known to be true and must be embraced on the basis of some epistemic state weaker than knowledge?

There are at least two reasons why this may well be *the* crucial question for Christian intellectuals to keep in mind as they do their work. For one thing, *Christianity claims to be a knowledge tradition,* and it places knowledge at the center of its proclamation and discipleship. The Old and New Testaments, including the teachings of Jesus, claim not merely that Christianity is true, but that a variety of its moral and religious assertions can be known to be true.

Second, *knowledge is the basis of responsible action in society.* Dentists, not lawyers, have the authority to place their hands in our mouths because they have the relevant knowledge on the basis of which they may act responsibly. If Christian scholars do little to deflect the view that theological and ethical assertions are merely parts of a belief tradition which simply adds a "theological perspective" to an otherwise unperturbed secular topic and fails to convey knowledge, then they inadvertently contribute to the marginalization of Christianity. They do so precisely because they fail to rebut the contemporary tendency to rob the Christian faith of the very thing that gives it the authority necessary to prevent that marginalization, *viz.*, its legitimate claim to give us moral and religious knowledge. Both in and out of the church, Jesus has been lost as an intellectual authority. Christian intellectuals should embrace the authority of Jesus and carry out their academic vocation in light of this fact.

I agree with those who see a three-way worldview struggle in academic and popular culture among ethical monotheism (especially Christian theism), postmodernism, and scientific naturalism. As Christian intellectuals seek to promote Christianity as a knowledge tradition in their academic discipline, they should keep in mind the impact of their work on this triumvirate. Both space considerations and my own view of priorities forbid me to say much about postmodernism here. I recognize it is a variegated tunic with many nuances. But to the degree that postmodernism denies the objectivity of reality, truth, value, reason (in its epistemic if not psychological sense); to the degree that it rejects dichotomous thinking about real/unreal, true/false, rational/irrational, right/wrong; to the degree that it takes intentionality to create the objects of consciousness, to that degree it should be resisted by Christian intellectuals.

Scientific naturalism also comes in many varieties but, very roughly, a major form of it is the view that the spatio-temporal cosmos containing physical objects studied by the hard sciences is all there is. It also maintains that the hard sciences are either the only source of knowledge or else vastly superior in proffering epistemically justified beliefs compared to non-scientific fields. In connection with scientific naturalism, some have argued that the rise of modern science has contributed to the loss of intellectual authority in those fields like ethics and religion that, supposedly, are not subject to the types of testing and experimentation employed in the hard sciences. Rightly or wrongly, there are three ways that science has been perceived as a threat to the intellectual credibility of Christianity:

> 1. Some scientific claims call into question certain interpretations of biblical texts (e.g., Genesis 1 and 2) or certain theological beliefs (e.g., that humans have souls or are made in the image of God).

2. Some scientific claims, if correct, demote certain arguments for the existence of God (e.g., if natural, evolutionary processes can explain the origin or development of life, then we do not "need" to postulate a Creator/Designer to explain these things). There may be other reasons for believing in God, but the advances of science have robbed Christians of a number of arguments that used to be effective.

3. The progress of science, compared to other disciplines like philosophy or theology, justifies scientism either by the view that science and science *alone* offers true, justified beliefs (*strong* scientism) or that while other fields may offer true, justified beliefs, in general, the degree of certainty in science *vastly outweighs* what these other fields offer (*weak* scientism). As evolutionary naturalist George Gaylord Simpson put it:

> There is neither need nor excuse for postulation of nonmaterial intervention in the origin of life, the rise of man, or any other part of the long history of the material cosmos. Yet the origin of that cosmos and the causal principles of its history remain unexplained and inaccessible to science. Here is hidden the First Cause sought by theology and philosophy. The First Cause is not known and I suspect it will never be known to living man. We may, if we are so inclined, worship it in our own ways, but we certainly do not comprehend it."[2]

Now Christians must respond to these three problem areas. One solution is the *complementarity* view according to which propositions, theories, or methodologies in theology and other disciplines may involve two different, complementary, non-interacting approaches to the same reality. On this view, theology and science interact much like the color and shape descriptions of an apple. Theology and science (or, for that matter, any discipline besides theology) interact in an *additive* way such that the whole truth is the sum of the contributions of both but neither has direct, straightforward implications for the other. In my opinion, the complementarian approach is inadequate as a total integrative model because, among other things, *it contributes to the widespread philosophical naturalism that dominates much of the contemporary academy and broader culture.* As Philip E. Johnson has pointed out:

> Politically astute scientific naturalists feel no hostility toward those religious leaders who implicitly accept the key naturalistic doctrine that supernatural powers do not actually affect the course of nature. . . . The most sophisticated naturalists realize that it is better just to say that statements about God are "religious" and hence incapable of being more than expressions of subjective feeling. It would be pretty ridiculous, after all, to make a big deal out of proving that Zeus and Apollo do not really exist.[3]

Elsewhere, Johnson observes:

> the conflict between the naturalistic worldview and the Christian supernaturalistic worldview goes all the way down. It cannot be papered over by superficial compromises. . . . It cannot be mitigated by reading the Bible figuratively rather than literally. . . . There is no satisfactory way to bring two such fundamentally different stories together, although various bogus intellectual systems offer a superficial compromise to those who are willing to overlook a logical contradiction or two. A clear thinker simply has to go one way or another.[4]

Johnson's remarks serve as a reminder that Christian complementarians run the risk of achieving an integration between science and Christian theism at the price of placing the epistemological authority and certain important metaphysical claims of Christianity in some private, upper story. Whether intentional or not, when employed too broadly, the complementarity approach contributes to the scientism that controls contemporary culture. Thereby, it inadvertently fosters a separation of the secular and sacred due to the fact that careful biblical exegesis does very little intellectual work in the areas of study where complementarity is employed. The effect of this is to marginalize Christian doctrine in the marketplace of ideas.

In my view, Christian complementarians give up too much intellectual ground too quickly in light of the philosophical naturalism's cultural sway. I am neither a sociologist nor the son of one, but I still opine that philosophical naturalism is sustained in the academy and broader culture by sociological—and not distinctly rational—factors. In my discipline of philosophy, signs indicate that important figures are finally acknowledging this. For example, naturalist Thomas Nagel has recently written:

> In speaking of the fear of religion, . . . , I am talking about . . . the fear of religion itself. I speak from experience, being strongly subject to this fear myself. . . . I want atheism to be true and am made uneasy by the fact that some of the most intelligent and well-informed people I know are religious believers. It isn't just that I don't believe in God and, naturally, hope that I'm right in my belief. It's that I hope there is no God! I don't want there to be a God; I don't want the universe to be like that. . . . My guess is that this cosmic authority problem is not a rare condition and that it is responsible for much of the scientism and reductionism of our time. One of the tendencies it supports is the ludicrous overuse of evolutionary biology to explain everything about life, including everything about the human mind.[5]

Along similar lines, in his 1996 presidential address for the Pacific Division of the American Philosophical Association, Barry Stroud noted,

"Naturalism" seems to me in this and other respects rather like "world peace." Almost everyone swears allegiance to it, and is willing to march under its banner. But disputes can still break out about what is appropriate or acceptable to do in the name of that slogan. And like world peace, once you start specifying concretely exactly what it involves and how to achieve it, it becomes increasingly difficult to reach and to sustain a consistent and exclusive "naturalism."[6]

I know these remarks are terse and controversial, and in the future I shall try to develop and defend my understanding of the nature and limitations of a complementarity view of integration. For now, I turn to a brief presentation of the epistemic tasks of integration and the models used to carry out those tasks.

Epistemic Tasks for Integration

The word "integration" means to form or blend into a whole, to unite. The human intellect naturally seeks to find the unity that is behind diversity and, in fact, coherence is an important mark of rationality. In conceptual integration, one's theological beliefs, especially those derived from careful biblical exegesis, are blended and unified with propositions judged to be justifiably believed as true from other sources into a coherent, intellectually satisfying worldview. One of the goals of integration is to maintain or increase both the conceptual relevance of and epistemological justification for Christian theism. To repeat St. Augustine's advice, "We must show our Scriptures not to be in conflict with whatever [our critics] can demonstrate about the nature of things from reliable sources."[7] We may distinguish three different aspects of the epistemological side of integration: direct defense, polemics, and Christian explanation.

1. *Direct Defense.* In direct defense, one engages in integration with the primary intent of enhancing or maintaining directly the epistemic justification of Christian theism or some proposition taken to be explicit within or entailed by it, especially those aspects of a Christian worldview relevant to one's own discipline. Specific attention should be given to

topics that are intrinsically important to mere Christianity or currently under fire in one's field of study. Hereafter, I will simply refer to these issues as "Christian theism." I do so for brevity's sake. "Christian theism" should be taken to include specific views about a particular area of study that one takes to be relevant to the integrative task.

There are two basic forms of direct defense, one negative and one positive.[8] The less controversial of the two is a negative direct defense where one attempts to remove defeaters to Christian theism. If you have a justified belief regarding some proposition P, a defeater is something that weakens or removes that justification. Defeaters come in two types:[9] rebutting defeaters and undercutting defeaters. A rebutting defeater gives justification for believing not-P-in this case, that Christian theism is false. For example, attempts to show that the biblical concept of the family is dysfunctional and false or that homosexuality is causally necessitated by genes or brain states and that, therefore, it is not a proper object for moral appraisal are cases of rebutting defeaters. An undercutting defeater does not give justification for believing not-P, but rather seeks to remove or weaken justification for believing P in the first place. Critiques of the arguments for God's existence are examples of undercutting defeaters. When defeaters are raised against Christian theism, a negative defense seeks either to rebut or undercut those defeaters.

By contrast, a positive direct defense is an attempt to build a positive case for Christian theism. Arguments for the existence of God, objective morality, the existence of the soul, the value and nature of virtue ethics, and the possibility and knowability of miracles are examples. This task for integration is not accepted by all Christian intellectuals. For example, various species of what may be loosely called Reformed epistemology run the gamut from seeing a modest role for a positive direct defense to an outright rejection of this type of activity in certain areas, e.g., justifying belief in God and the authority of Holy Scripture.

2. *Philosophical Polemics.* In philosophical polemics, one seeks to criticize views that rival Christian theism in one way or another. Critiques of scientific naturalism, physicalism, pantheism, and normative ethical relativism are all cases of philosophical polemics.

3. *Theistic explanation.* Christian theists ought to be about the business of exploring the world in light of their worldview and, more specifically, of using their theistic beliefs as explanations of the various relevant

features regarding the intellectual landscape. Suppose we have a set of items x_i through x_n that stand in need of explanation and we offer some explanations E as an adequate or even best explanation of the items. In such a case, E explains x_i through x_n, and this fact provides some degree of confirmation for E. For example, if a certain intrinsic genre statement explains the various data of a biblical text, then this fact offers some confirmation for the belief that the statement is the correct interpretation of that text.

We should seek to solve intellectual problems and shed light on areas of puzzlement by utilizing the explanatory power of our worldview. For example, for those who accept the existence of natural moral law, the irreducibly mental nature of consciousness, natural human rights, or the fact that human flourishing follows from certain biblically mandated ethical and religious practices, the truth of Christian theism provides a good explanation of these phenomena. And this fact can provide some degree of confirmation for Christian theism.

Models Employed in Integration

When problem areas surface, there is a need for the Christian scholar to think hard about the issue in light of the need for strengthening the epistemic authority of Christian theism and placing it squarely within the plausibility structure of contemporary culture. Let us use the term "theology" to stand for any Christian idea that seems to be a part of a Christian worldview derived primarily from special revelation. When one addresses problems like these, there will emerge a number of different ways that theology can interact with an issue in a discipline outside theology. Here are some of the different ways that such interaction can take place.

> 1. *The Two Realms View.* Propositions, theories, or methodologies in theology and another discipline may involve two distinct, non-overlapping areas of investigation. For example, debates about angels or the extent of the atonement have little to do with organic chemistry. Similarly, it is of little interest to theology

whether a methane molecule has three or four hydrogen atoms in it.

2. *The Complementarity View.* Propositions, theories, or methodologies in theology and another discipline may involve two different, complementary, non-interacting approaches to the same reality.[10] Sociological aspects of church growth and certain psychological aspects of conversion may be sociological or psychological descriptions of certain phenomena that are complementary to a theological description of church growth or conversion.[11]

3. *The Direct Interaction View.* Propositions, theories, or methodologies in theology and another discipline may directly interact in such a way that either one area of study offers rational support for the other or one area of study raises rational difficulties for the other. For example, certain theological teachings about the existence of the soul raise rational problems for philosophical or scientific claims that deny the existence of the soul. The general theory of evolution raises various difficulties for certain ways of understanding the book of Genesis. Some have argued that the Big Bang theory tends to support the theological proposition that the universe had a beginning.

4. *The Presuppositions View.* Theology tends to support the presuppositions of another discipline and vice versa. Some have argued that many of the presuppositions of science (e.g. the existence of truth, the rational, orderly nature of reality, the adequacy of our sensory and cognitive faculties as tools suited for knowing the external world) make sense and are easy to justify given Christian theism, but are odd and without ultimate justification in a naturalistic world view. Similarly, some have argued that philosophical critiques of

epistemological skepticism and defenses of the existence of a real, theory-independent world and a correspondence theory of truth offer justification for some of the presuppositions of theology.

5. *The Practical Application View.* Theology fills out and adds details to general principles in another discipline and vice versa, and theology helps one practically apply principles in another discipline and vice versa. For example, theology teaches that fathers should not provoke their children to anger and psychology can add important details about what this means by offering information about family systems, the nature and causes of anger, etc. Psychology can devise various tests for assessing whether one is or is not a mature person and theology can offer a normative definition to psychology as to what a mature person is.

There is much work to be done by Christian scholars in the integrative task. Moreover, as we carry out this task in our own vocations, we should place a priority on the issue surfaced by a convergence of the intrinsic nature of Christianity and the current intellectual environment in its unfavorable aspects, viz., at showing that Christianity is a knowledge tradition and employing it as such. As we labor in this endeavor, we will want to keep in mind different epistemic tasks that focus our work, different models of integration available to us, and the role of our disciplines in the mission of concern to us all.

---

[1] Augustine, *De Genesi ad litteram* 1.21. Cited in Ernan McMullin, "How Should Cosmology Relate to Theology?" in *The Science and Theology in the Twentieth Century*, ed. Arthur R. Peacocke (Notre Dame: University of Notre Dame Press, 1981), 20.

[2] George Gaylord Simpson, *The Meaning of Evolution* (New York: Bantam Books, 1971), 252.

[3] Phillip E. Johnson, *Defeating Darwinism* (Downers Grove, Ill.: InterVarsity, 1997), 100-1.

[4] Ibid., 111.

[5] Thomas Nagel, *The Last Word* (New York: Oxford University Press, 1997), 130-31.

6 Barry Stroud, "The Charm of Naturalism," *Proceedings and Addresses of the American Philosophical Association* 70 (1996): 43-44.

7 Augustine, *De genesi ad litteram* 1.21.

8 See Ronald Nash, *Faith and Reason* (Grand Rapids: Zondervan, 1988), 14-18.

9 For a useful discussion of various types of defeaters, see John Pollock, *Contemporary Theories of Knowledge* (Totowa, N.J.: Rowman & Littlefield, 1986), 36-9; Ralph Baergen, *Contemporary Epistemology* (Fort Worth, Tex.: Hartcourt Brace and Company, 1995), 119-24.

10 Richard Bube has complained that my characterization of complementarity is confused and is actually a description of what he calls compartmentalization. See his *Putting it All Together* (Lanham, Md.: University Press of America, 1995), 168. Cf. chs. 6 and 10. For Bube, compartmentalization treats science and theology as different descriptions about different kinds of things with no common ground or possibility of conflict. Complementarity views science and theology as different descriptions of the same reality. Unfortunately, Bube is simply wrong in this complaint towards my position. What he calls compartmentalization is close to what I call the "two realms" view of integration and my description of complementarity is an accurate one. The source of Bube's confusion is revealing. I claim that the complementarity view eschews interaction between science and theology and Bube says that it embraces such interaction. However, Bube equivocates on what "interaction' means in this context. For me, it is "epistemic" interaction, roughly the same description of the same reality that can be in conflict or concord to varying degrees of strength. For Bube, interaction amounts to taking two different (non-interacting in my sense) perspectives and forming them into a whole. For example, a completely scientific description of the origin of life in natural terms could be described in theological terms as God's activity in bringing life into being. It is clear that his notion of interaction is not the one I deny in explicating complementarity.

11 I shall elaborate more on this approach in a subsequent paper: www.leaderu.com/aip/conference2.html.

Chapter Four

———∾∾∾———

ESSENTIALS OF POSTMODERNISM[1]

Stan Wallace

Stan Wallace works with InterVarsity's Graduate and Faculty Ministries as the Gulf States Area Director and serves as InterVarsity's Emerging Scholars Network Coordinator. He has done doctoral work in philosophy at Marquette University, and has published philosophical articles in professional journals such as the International Philosophical Quarterly and Philosophia Christi.

Abstract

"Via philosophical analysis, we find two fundamental theses that underlie postmodernism and are the flower bed out of which the rest of postmodernist thought grows. As such, it is appropriate to identify these two metaphysical theses as the essential features of postmodernism—the necessary and co-sufficient conditions under which a view may appropriately be defined as postmodern—for if they are consistently applied, one derives the other features of a postmodernist ideology. On the other hand, if one or both are denied, and a Realism regarding universals and/or a correspondence view regarding truth is embraced, the resultant view will clearly not be postmodern in nature."

EVEN A CURSORY GLANCE AT THE LITERATURE
in any field of study indicates that postmodernism and its implications
are much discussed in the academy. Much of the focus is on the *nature*
of postmodernism, and there are many diverse opinions on this topic.
Christians in academia must carefully analyze these diverse opinions and
seek a correct understanding of postmodernism in order to know how
to relate to this intellectual movement as Christian academics.

Though much is being written on the nature of postmodernism, it
appears that many of the analyses focus on what may be termed
"accidental properties"—properties that admittedly accompany much
postmodern thought, but are not essential to it. This chapter will briefly
discuss some of these accidental features; touch on the difficulties
that result from identifying these as necessary or essential features; go
on to offer what seem to be the necessary or essential features of
postmodernism; and compare these to the essential commitments of the
Christian worldview. The result is an understanding of postmodern
thought that allows us to embrace what is laudable and avoid what is
amiss in the postmodernist view.

Many definitions of postmodernism are "historical" in orientation.
Beginning with the reference to modernity in "postmodernity," this
approach seeks to define postmodernity in terms of what it rejects of
modernity. Many features of modernity have been identified, the most
prominent being its view of freedom, rationality, and progress.
Postmodernists eschew modernist views that inflate reason to the status
of an entirely independent, neutral, unbiased and objective instrument
with which truth can and will be found. Regarding progress, postmodernists
are quick to point out that, *contra* modernity, we are not "every day, in
every way, getting better and better," but rather in some cases are creating
survival-threatening conditions by the unbridled push toward technological
"progress." The same skepticism is applied to freedom. Whereas modernity
placed freedom or human autonomy as one of the highest values to be
embraced, the postmodernist suggests our freedom is an illusion; and, in

fact, we are determined by factors well beyond our control—be they race, gender, culture, etc.

It seems clear that at least these features of postmodernity are in some ways commensurate with the Christian worldview. For example, we too reject the rationalism of modernity with its disdain for divine revelation or anything "scandalous" to reason. We agree that sin entails certain noetic effects, diminishing our reasoning capacity and making it a bit more suspect that modernity would admit. We agree "progress" is not always good, e.g., the fact that we can clone a human being does not mean that we *should* do so. And we agree human progress will not lead us to "utopia"; this can only be achieved through life in and through the kingdom of God. We agree that we are not ultimately free and autonomous beings. The words of the Apostle Paul in Romans 3:23 remind us that we regularly sin and are constantly falling short of the glory of God—that is, his likeness.[2] Hence as Christians we find at least some, if not a great deal, of agreement and common ground with the postmodernist on these issues.

However, some have taken these features to be the essential features of postmodernity, and, seeing the parallels to the Christian worldview, have embraced postmodernism as fully compatible with Christianity. I believe this to be a grave error, due at least in part to the assumption that these features of postmodernity are essential and not accidental elements of postmodernity. In fact, via philosophical inspection it becomes clear that these points of commonality derive from radically different and antithetical metaphysical commitments, which serve to identify the essence of postmodernity and mark it as essentially and deeply anti-Christian.[3] To those essential features of the postmodern and Christian worldviews we now turn.

Foundational to each person's understanding of reality (whatever that is taken to be) stands a "metaphysic." *The Cambridge Dictionary of Philosophy* defines metaphysics as "the philosophical investigation of the nature, constitution, and structure of reality."[4] One's metaphysic ultimately defines and guides thought, action, values, etc. Underlying postmodernism is a metaphysic which ultimately unites all other seemingly diverse strands of thought within that lineage, and as such may aptly be identified as the essence of postmodernism. This essential postmodern metaphysic maintains a thoroughgoing nominalism and a rejection of truth as correspondence to a mind-independent world.

Feature #1: Nominalism and the Rejection of Realism

First, postmodernism is essentially nominalistic. This may be best understood by comparing it to the alternative: metaphysical Realism (hereafter simply "Realism").[5] Realism maintains that universals do exist—entities that are transcendent (i.e., exist apart from, or transcend the individual and culture), objective (not mind-dependent), and capable of being multiply-exemplified ("had" by more than one individual thing at the same time). This final point is often identified as the essence of Realism. Using the property "whiteness" as an example, Reinhardt Grossmann summarizes the position:

> Is the whiteness of the two billiard balls literally the same? Is there just one entity which is exemplified by both balls? Or does each ball have its own whiteness? This is the so-called problem of universals . . . . Philosophers who believe that the color of billiard ball A is the very same as that of billiard ball B are called realists. Those who deny this are called *nominalists*.[6]

As examples of such universals Realists point to, for example, moral values, natures, and propositions. Realism maintains that such things as goodness and justice exist and are transcendent, objective and multiply-exemplifiable. The same is true of human nature and propositions (such as the laws of logic), according to the Realist.[7]

By contrast, Nominalism maintains that no universals exist, but rather all that exists are particular, discrete things. Nothing is transcendent. Hence it follows that such things as moral values, human nature, and propositions are created by the individual (or collectively by the society), not discovered as existent "out there." As such, they are not objective and absolute, but rather subjective, bound to the individual and/or culture for their existence and validity. We find this metaphysic echoing throughout the writings of the leading proponents of postmodernism. Concerning values, Michel Foucault wrote: "The domination of certain men over others leads to the differentiation of values; class domination *generates* the idea of liberty . . . ."[8] Concerning propositions, Jacques Derrida states, "The absence of a transcendental signified extends the domain and the play of significations infinitely,"[9] thus echoing the words of Nietzsche, "There are no facts, only interpretations."[10] Again, in reference to natures Foucault writes,

> Why does Nietzsche challenge the pursuit of the origin (*Ursprung*) . . . ? First, because it is an attempt to capture the exact essence of things . . . because this search assumes the existence of immobile forms that precede the eternal world of accident and succession. . . . However . . . there is "something altogether different" behind things: not a timeless and essential secret, but the secret that *they have no essence*. . . .[11]

In sum, the nominalistic metaphysic of postmodernity denies the transcendence, objectivity and multiple-exemplification of moral values, natures and propositions. The important point here is that for the postmodernist there are *no* universals. Realists disagree as to just how many types of things are universals, but are in agreement that some such properties exist as universals, as illustrated above. The postmodernist stands against this as a thoroughgoing nominalist: *there are no universals whatsoever.*

Feature #2: Rejection of Truth as Correspondence

Furthermore, we may identify a second essential feature of postmodernism: the rejection of truth as "correspondence." On a "correspondence" view, truth is understood to obtain in virtue of correspondence between a proposition (such as "Snow is white") and the state of affairs in (mind-independent) reality (snow really being white "out there" in the world). Such a view is squarely rejected by postmodernity. For the postmodernist no appeal is made to an external "reality" beyond the individual and/or culture, which grounds a proposition as "true." Hence truth is ultimately grounded in the individual or culture. As Richard Rorty has stated,

> Those who wish to ground solidarity in objectivity . . .
> have to construe truth as correspondence to reality. . . .
> By contrast, those who wish to reduce objectivity to
> solidarity . . .view truth as, in William James' phrase,
> what is good for us to believe. *So they do not need an*
> *account of a relation between beliefs and objects called*
> *"correspondence"* . . . .[12]

In the words of Nietzsche, to whom many postmodernists look for inspiration, truth is

> a mobile army of metaphors, metonyms, and
> anthromorphisms—in short a sum of *human* relations,
> which have been enhanced, transposed, and
> embellished poetically and rhetorically and which after
> long use *seem* firm, canonical, and obligatory to a people.[13]

Foucault would concur, writing that the "*forceful appropriation* of things necessary to survival and the *imposition* of a duration *not intrinsic* to them account for the *origin* of logic."[14]

Once understood, it is not difficult to see the ubiquity of this metaphysic in the outworkings of postmodern thought. While space does not permit a detailed elucidation, several examples should suffice to illustrate the point. Take, for example, the postmodern view of rationality, which follows immediately from this metaphysic. Following from a rejection of truth as correspondence to the state of affairs in mind-independent reality (and thus the positing of reason and "truth" as individually- or culturally-determined), one can easily understand why it is anathema to assume to have "objective" truth in the postmodernist milieu. Indeed, such assertions are paramount to cultural imperialism, the violent imposition of one's subjective, cultural dispositions on others so as to conquer and subjugate. The same is true concerning deconstruction and the hermeneutics of suspicion: the greatest of all errors is to assume to have the one "true," "correct" or "preferred" interpretation of a text, for to do so is to assume truth is objective and knowable. Given the postmodern metaphysic such is certainly not the case, and those who assume such an objective interpretation of a text has been obtained (or is even possible) must be motivated to claim as much due to political or social factors—ultimately the desire to have power and authority over others. As Foucault summarizes,

> Truth is a thing of this world: it is produced only by virtue of multiple forms of constraint. And it induces regular effects of power. Each society has its regime of truth, its "general politics" of truth: that is, the types of discourse which it accepts and makes function as true . . . . [15]

Furthermore, this postmodern metaphysic explains the motivation to reject metanarratives, which by definition are comprehensive worldviews understood to be the accurate and "true" understanding of reality. Such metanarratives as religious traditions (e.g., Christianity, Islam, Buddhism) and philosophical systems (e.g., Marxism, humanism, modernity) are to be unequivocally eschewed due to their claim of having truth that transcends the individual or cultural; truly knowing the framework of reality as it actually is diametrically opposes the postmodernist metaphysic. Jean-François Lyotard summarizes: "Simplifying to the extreme, I define *postmodern* as incredulity toward metanarratives."[16] Finally, following from the rejection of an objectively-grounded human nature, it follows that one's personal identity must be grounded not in virtue of being human *per se*, but rather in terms of more narrow groupings, such as ethnicity, gender, sexual orientation, and so on. Similar examples of the outworking of this metaphysic are to be found in the various other doctrines often associated with postmodernism.

In summary, I suggest a far more adequate definition of postmodernity is to be found via "philosophical" analysis, rather than "historical" analysis. Via philosophical analysis, we find two fundamental theses which underlie postmodernism and are the flower bed out of which the rest of postmodernist thought grows. As such, it is appropriate to identify these two metaphysical theses as the essential features of postmodernism—the necessary and co-sufficient conditions under which a view may appropriately be defined as postmodern—for if they are consistently applied, one derives the other features of a postmodernist ideology. On the other hand, if one or both are denied, and a Realism regarding

STAN WALLACE

universals and/or a correspondence view regarding truth is embraced, the resultant view will clearly not be postmodern in nature.

However, it is precisely in regards to these two commitments that postmodernism and the Christian worldview are at odds. First, the Christian worldview clearly assumes Realism concerning values, natures and propositions. For instance, the moral rightness of loving God or acting justly are posited as values that transcend individuals and cultures, are transcendent and objective, and are multiply-exemplified throughout cultures and times (the *same* value can and has been exemplified by *many* people at *many* times). Likewise regarding natures: the Christian worldview assumes such a thing as human nature exists (for the incarnation was the taking on of something real—a *real* human nature), and the nature assumed by Christ was the same nature as that of other humans, such that Christ was *truly* a human being and thus an equal and adequate substitute. As Hebrews 2:14 states, ". . . he too shared in their humanity so that by his death he might destroy him who holds the power of death."[17] Finally, the same may be said regarding propositions: the Christian world view accepts these as universals. Such things as theological propositions (e.g., "God exists, "God is good") are taken to be true, not subjectively, but objectively, and multiply-exemplified. That is, the *same* proposition can be had by many minds at one time such that inter-subjective communication is possible; it obtains across time and cultures such that dialogue with those of other times and cultures is possible.

Secondly, a correspondence view of truth appears to be most consistent and even assumed by the Christian worldview. For example, propositions such as "In the beginning God created the heavens and the earth" (Genesis 1:1) and "Christ died for our sins according to the Scriptures, that he was buried, that he was raised on the third day . . ." (1 Cor. 15:3-4) are understood by Christians as being true, and true in virtue of their accurately describing the actual or real state of affairs. As such, the Christian would assert that such propositions would be true even if no (human) minds ever entertained such propositions. For example, God surely could have created the heavens and the earth without populating it with human knowers, in which case it would still be true that God created the heavens and the earth, but that truth would in no way be dependent on (human) minds. Thus in the Christian worldview, truth is not mind-dependent and hence subjective, but rather mind independent, and objective.

Conclusion

Therefore, having identified the essence of postmodernist thought and the Christian world view we may conclude that (1) though there are points of common ground between the Christian and postmodernist views of the world that should not be ignored, (2) ultimately the Christian and postmodern metaphysic are diametrically opposed one to the other, and thus (3) we must be careful and reflective as we engage these ideas in the academy. The details of such engagement will be as varied as our disciplines and universities. Yet these fundamental metaphysical issues transcend the particulars of disciplines and universities, and as such give us a foothold: a place to begin the process of seeking to embrace truth and avoid error concerning these most important issues.

---

[1] I wish to thank J. P. Moreland for helpful comments on an earlier draft of this paper.

[2] See Douglas Moo, *The Epistle to the Romans* NICNT (Grand Rapids: Eerdmans, 1996), 226.

[3] For example, the believer may find the theistically-sympathetic views of the "postmodernist" author Emmanuel Levinas refreshing, but this tends to be the exception.

[4] *Cambridge Dictionary of Philosophy*, ed. Robert Audi (Cambridge: Cambridge University Press, 1995), s.v. "metaphysics."

[5] A third option often mentioned "between" these two positions is conceptualism: Universals transcend the particulars, though they exist universally only in one's mind as concepts. Yet in my view this option ultimately reduced to a nominalistic view if these mental "universals" are taken to be nothing more than individual ideas that have no ontic status outside the individual thinker (and hence are not multiply exemplifiable), or reduces to Realism if these concepts are taken to be entities with mind-independent status and are thus multiply-exemplifiable. Therefore, though there is a great deal of debate on these issues, for our purposes it is sufficient to identify Nominalism and Realism as the two options most germane to our attempt to define postmodernism.

[6] Reinhardt Grossmann, *The Existence of the World: An Introduction to Ontology* (New York: Routledge, 1992), 12. See also James Porter Moreland, *Universals, Qualities, and Quality Instances: A Defense of Realism* (Lanham, Md.: University Press of America, 1985).

[7] I have focused on those entities most widely agreed to be universals by Realists. There are other candidates, about which there is more debate concerning their status. These include colors (e.g., red), shapes (e.g., triangularity), aesthetic values (e.g., beauty) and numbers (represented by the numerals "1," "2," etc.).

[8] Michel Foucault, "Nietzsche, Genealogy, History" in *Language, Counter-Memory, Practice: Selected Essays and Articles,* ed. with intro. by Donald F. Bouchard; trans. Donald F. Bouchard and Sherry Simon (Ithaca, N.Y.: Cornell University Press, 1977), 150 (italics added).

[9] Jacques Derrida, *Writing and Difference,* trans. Alan Bass (Chicago: University of Chicago Press, 1978), 280.

[10] Nietzsche, *The Will to Power,* trans. Walter Kaufmann and R. Hollingdale (New York: Random House, 1968), 267.

[xi] Michel Foucault, "Nietzsche, Genealogy, History" in *Language, Counter-Memory, Practice,* 142. He goes on to state, "Nothing in man—not even his body—is sufficiently stable to serve as the basis for self-recognition or for understanding other men."

[11] Michel Foucault, "Nietzsche, Genealogy, History" in *Language, Counter-Memory, Practice,* 153 (italics added).

[12] Richard Rorty, "Solidarity or Objectivity?" in *Objectivity, Relativism, and Truth* (New York: Cambridge University Press, 1991), 22 (italics added).

[13] Nietzsche, "On Truth and Lie in an Extra-Moral Sense," in *The Portable Nietzsche,* trans. and ed. Walter Kaufmann (New York: Viking Press, 1980), 46-7 (italics added).

[14] Michel Foucault, "Nietzsche, Genealogy, History" in *Language, Counter-Memory, Practice,* 150 (italics added).

[15] Michel Foucault, "Truth and Power" in *Power/Knowledge: Selected Interviews and Other Writings,* 1972-1977, ed. Colin Gordon; trans. Colin Gordon, et al. (New York: Pantheon Books, 1980), 131. Elsewhere Foucault writes, "This demagogy [assumption of objective historical analysis], of course, must be masked . . . . under the cloak of universals. As the demagogue is obliged to invoke truth, laws of essences, and eternal necessity, the historian must invoke objectivity, the accuracy of facts, and the permanence of the past." Michel Foucault, "Nietzsche, Genealogy, History" in *Language, Counter-Memory, Practice,* 158.

[16] Jean-François Lyotard, *The Postmodern Condition: A Report on Knowledge,* trans. Geoff Bennington and Brian Massumi (Minneapolis: University of Minnesota Press, 1984), xxiv.

[17] See also Philippians 2:7: Jesus "made himself nothing, *taking the very nature* of a servant . . ." (italics added).

PART II:

*PHILOSOPHICAL RESPONSES
TO CURRENT CHALLENGES*

Chapter Five

———

PRACTICAL RESPONSES TO RELATIVISM AND POSTMODERNISM: PART I

J. Budziszewski

J. Budziszewski (Ph.D., Yale) teaches government and philosophy at the University of Texas at Austin. Besides numerous journal articles, he has written a half dozen books including Written on the Heart: The Case for Natural Law (InterVarsity) and The Revenge of Conscience: Politics and the Fall of Man (Spence). His newest book is The Beginning of Wisdom (Spence).

Abstract

"Not many people are consistent either in maintaining relativism or in rejecting it. What we find in their thinking is not pure relativism, but partial relativism. In some cases, as in the postmodernist version of relativism, the relativism cannot be pure because of its sheer incoherency."

M Y AIM IS ENTIRELY PRACTICAL: TO consider how we can respond to relativism and its relatives when we encounter them among students and colleagues. Although the various and sundry moral skepticisms, noncognitivisms, and postmodernisms are not precisely the same, they do bear a family resemblance, and in this essay I treat them as a group.

The Classical Christian View of Morality

The crucial features of any view of morality are how it regards the source of morality, the authority of morality, and our knowledge of morality. As to its source, the classical Christian view is that moral law derives its authority from God and is reflected in the design of His creation. This doesn't mean that it is arbitrary; it is rooted in His eternal goodness. Nor does it *seem* to us *arbitrary*, because it meshes with the way we have been put together, and we discover it in the deep structure of our own created conscience. So the source of moral law is God as creator and lawgiver.

As to the rightness of the moral law and our knowledge of it, we hold that the foundational moral principles—principles like "love God," "love your neighbor," "do not murder," "do not commit adultery," and "give to people what they deserve rather than merely what you feel like giving them"—are "the same for all, both as to rectitude and as to knowledge." This phrase, from Thomas Aquinas, means that they are both right for everyone and known to everyone. Many people who would agree that the basic moral principles are right for everyone deny that they are known to everyone. Classically, Christianity has taken a stronger view. We may not know every detail of the moral law, but we cannot fail to know its greatest and most general laws. As St. Paul wrote, a certain knowledge of right and wrong is "written on the heart." It can be repressed, denied, or buried, but it cannot be annihilated.

Relativism and Postmodernism

In most forms, relativism denies all three points of the classical Christian view of morality. It denies that the source of moral law is God, denies that the foundational moral principles are right for everyone, and denies that they are known to everyone. Concerning its *source*, relativists say that morality has no transcendent source; people make it up. Concerning its *rightness*, they don't necessarily deny that there *is* such a thing as rightness—for instance, a relativist might say that something is "right for me" or "right for us"—but they refuse to admit that anything is right for all. Judge Richard Posner, for example, says morality is "local" rather than universal. And, of course, something which is not right for all cannot be known to all. So relativists deny the transcendence, the universal rightness, and the universal knowledge of moral law, all three points that Christians affirm.

Postmodernism is a contemporary variety of moral relativism. Simply put, it is the notion that no one gets the Big Story right about anything—indeed that perhaps there is no Big Story. Of course, postmodernists make a tacit exception for themselves; their Big Story *is* that no one gets the Big Story right about anything, and they *do* think they have it right. Postmodernism is usually described as a philosophical theory, but it really denies the possibility of philosophical theory. I think it is better described as a cultural mood. Although the mood of our own culture is postmodern, very few people have even heard the term "postmodernism." Surprisingly few university students have heard it. Fewer still could tell you what postmodernism is; fewer still could name a single postmodern writer. Certainly not many of them have been reading their works and thinking, "Yes, that's right."

If no one gets the Big Story right about anything, then no one gets the Big Story right about morality. That is why postmodernism is a form of moral relativism; in fact, it radicalizes it. Postmodernism says about *all* knowledge what garden-variety moral relativism says only about *moral* knowledge. It is an *epistemological* relativism. The garden-variety moral relativist says, "Right for you but not for me," but postmodernists go further by saying, "*True* for you but not for me," speaking not only of moral truth but of every kind of truth.

There have been views something like present-day moral relativism as long as there has been systematic moral reflection on this planet, and there have been views something like present-day postmodernism too. Socrates argued against the relativists of his day, who were called Sophists. No doubt you have heard the slogan "Man is the measure of all things." That motto comes from the Sophist Protagoras. Ultimately, it denies reality. Man is the measure of all things, but man has no fixed nature. Man measures all things by his words, but words have no fixed meanings. Language is not an instrument for finding truth, but an instrument for changing it. Those who can master language, master all. It was a good creed for rogues, and commends itself to tyrants in every age.

Logically, postmodernism is easy to refute. If the postmodernist says, "Nothing is true for everyone," we can ask: "Is *that* statement true for everyone?" I have yet to hear any postmodernist give a half-decent answer to this question. Most merely talk faster to cover up their incoherency.

In fact, incoherency is a key concept for understanding the postmodern variety of relativism, but I had better explain the term. We all know what *inconsistency* is. I am inconsistent if I say, "This chair is blue—*and* this chair is not blue." The first statement and the second statement contradict each other. Inconsistency, or contradiction, is the most obvious form of incoherency. But it is not the only form, and it is not the form that postmodernists tend to be guilty of committing. Generally speaking, an intellectual position is incoherent whenever it cuts out the ground from underneath, no matter how it does this. The old Looney Toons cartoons provoked laughter with characters who sawed off the very tree limbs they were sitting on, or who ran off cliffs, pedaling their feet out in midair for a few seconds before realizing that there was nothing beneath their feet to hold them up. That is what incoherency is like.

Here are some examples of incoherency that do *not* involve inconsistency. A postmodernist might say: "I want you to understand this: You can never figure out what any speaker means." Yet he expects you to figure out what *he* means. This isn't literally inconsistent because he hasn't said "I want you to understand this, but also I want you not to." However, it is incoherent because by his own principles, what he expects you to do is impossible. Here is another example: Someone says, "No meaningful proposition can be expressed." He hasn't explicitly contradicted himself by saying "No meaningful proposition can be expressed, *and some* meaningful statement can be expressed." Yet he may as well have done so, because by the very act of expressing the statement, with the expectation that you will understand him, he *presupposes* that some meaningful statement can be expressed after all. Similarly with the statement "There is no universal truth." It expresses a universal negative which the speaker does suppose to be true; its content is contradicted by its presupposition.

Although it is easy to point out incoherency, getting someone to admit it is more difficult. One thing that makes it difficult is the postmodernist predilection for obscure language. If you can't even understand what a fellow is saying, you may be afraid to take him on. You may think that exposing his intellectual pretensions is beyond your ability, and that in order to do so you would have to be a high-flying expert in the postmodernist's field. But this is rarely the case.

C.S. Lewis said that a good test of whether you understand something is whether you can express it in uneducated language, in street talk. Over the years both as a graduate student and then as a teacher to scholarly and popular audiences, I have found a number of very interesting things. I have not yet met a postmodernist who can express postmodernism in street talk. It's not that it can't be done. Postmodernists sometimes define postmodernism as "suspicion of metanarratives." I've translated that into street talk already: it is refusing to believe that anyone gets the Big Story right about anything (except for the postmodernist, who thinks this *is* the Big Story.) But you will have to travel far to meet a postmodernist who will provide a translation into street talk himself. The problem is not a lack of education or of intellectual capacity. The problem is that once postmodernism is translated into street talk, anyone can see how silly it is. That is just what the postmodernist doesn't want anyone—including himself—to understand. So don't wait for relativists and postmodernists to provide translations; provide them yourself. You will be surprised how much progress you make in the conversation once you do.

What does postmodernism mean to the postmodernist who does not know that he is a postmodernist? What does it mean to the pop star whom culture critics praise for his postmodernist lyrics, but who has never heard the expression and perhaps cannot pronounce a word longer than three syllables?

As a cultural mood, postmodernism is simply *the habit of thinking that nothing holds together, that everything is in pieces.* That's the postmodern way of looking at things. A postmodernist, for instance, thinks that truth is fragmented. Instead of believing in a truth which is the same for everyone, he believes in stories which are different for everyone (except that he calls them "narratives" or "discourses"). He also thinks personality is fragmented. Instead of believing that each of us has a soul, a self, an I, that keeps its identity and is responsible for everything that it does, he believes that we play roles—one day the role of nice girl, the next day the role of tramp; one day the role of concerned citizen, the next day the role of "too cool to care." Personality for him dissolves into a succession of masks, and if you ask who is wearing the masks, he says you don't get it. Bill Clinton was sometimes called the first postmodern President because every week, every day, sometimes every hour, we seemed to get a different Clinton.

Besides thinking that truth is fragmented, and that personality is fragmented, the postmodernist thinks life itself is fragmented. He doesn't believe that life is going anywhere, that it has a theme, that it is "about" anything—his life, or your life either. But there is a crevice in this view, a crack into which we can drive in a wedge and split it open. You see, even the postmodernist has grasped hold of a little bit of truth. Note that I say "a little bit." They don't have much of it, and they are unable to give coherent expression even to the bit which they do have, yet—however small and however incoherently expressed—a grain of truth is here. Indeed, there has to be. Just as every vice is a parasite on a virtue, and just as everything bad is the pollution of something good, so also every error involves the distortion of something that is true—even postmodernism. The grain of truth is this: If you live apart from the Redeemer, then truth really will seem fragmented because you won't be able to make sense of things. If you live apart from the Redeemer, then personality really will seem fragmented because you won't know who you really are. And if you live apart from the Redeemer, then life really will seem fragmented because you will be unable to grasp its meaning and may simply give up trying. So as a description of what it is like, subjectively, to be fallen, postmodernism "ain't half-bad." It fails only as a description of the objective reality that God has made.

Postmodernism is much more difficult to defeat as a mood than as a proposition. It is easy to show that postmodernism is incoherent, but the postmodernist may strike a pose of not caring whether he is incoherent. But it *is* a pose; so don't be taken in. When someone tells me that he can do without meaning and coherency, I respond, "You know as well as I do that the longing for meaning and coherency is deep-set in every mind, yours as well as mine. So my question for you is this: *What is it that you want so badly that you are willing to give up even meaning and coherency to have it?*"

Relativism Is Rarely Absolute

Before discussing manifestations of relativism in the academy, I want to consider pure vs. partial relativism. The other day I read an article by a secularist in defense of his secular worldview. He wrote: "You know, we are accused all the time of being relativists," adding, "I don't even know any relativists. That's straw man. There aren't any relativists. In fact, in philosophy, there has been a renaissance of moral realism."

While his assertion about the discipline of philosophy is accurate, he was telling only half of the story. Not many people are consistent either in maintaining relativism or in rejecting it. What we find in their thinking is not pure relativism, but partial relativism. In some cases, as in the postmodernist version of relativism, the relativism cannot be pure because of its sheer incoherency. To be sure there are some versions of relativism that can be stated without incoherency, but these are not the versions we tend to find in people's minds. We find instead a confusion of relativist and non-relativist elements. This is not only true of people on the street but of our colleagues, our students, and the administrators of the schools in which we teach. All too often the mixture of relativism and non-relativism turns up in the thinking of Christians. If we are not careful, we may find it in our own thinking too.

Consider first the person who *does* think of himself as a relativist. He may begin by telling you "There are no *oughts*, no rights and wrongs that hold universally!" But then he follows up by saying "And that's why everyone *ought* to be tolerant!" Do you see the inconsistency?

"Tolerance is a virtue because there are no virtues." It amazes me how many variations on this argument I hear in my own field of ethical and political philosophy. The relativist mixes an element of moral affirmation with his denial of the possibility of moral affirmation. Psychologically, I think relativists have to do this. If they were really consistent in denying universal right and wrong, they could not make their relativism plausible even to themselves.

Consider next the person who *denies* being a relativist. He may begin by telling you "Morality expresses rules which hold for everyone." But when the subject turns to sex, then suddenly he says, "That may be right for you, but not for me." Do you see the inconsistency? Another example is the person proclaims the importance of universal moral rules—but who limits them to platitudes without fixed meaning, like "Be responsible." Just as most relativists mix non-relativist elements into their thinking, many people who do not consider themselves relativists mix relativist elements in their thinking. One must tread carefully.

Relativism in the Academy

Let's talk about how relativism manifests itself in our disciplines and on our campuses. First we need to realize that relativism is by no means limited to the liberal arts and the social sciences. Pervading almost all of the disciplines, for example, is the fact-value distinction. When I was an undergraduate, I was taught the fact-value distinction as an undisputed and indisputable truth: Facts were respectable to study because they were objective; values weren't respectable to study because they were subjective. Values were supposed to include not only ideas like "Vanilla is the best flavor of ice cream" (which really are subjective) but also ideas like "It is wrong to deliberately take the life of an innocent human being" (which aren't). So the fact-value distinction is merely another manifestation of relativism, supporting the prejudice that moral principles are purely personal. I was two-thirds of the way through graduate school before anyone ever suggested to me that a *reason* could be given for a moral judgment—that rational argumentation was possible about whether it was true or false.

Another manifestation of relativism is the replacement of reasoning-language ("I think," "I judge," "I conclude") with feeling-language ("I feel"). This is deadly. I don't allow feeling language in my classroom because it is merely subjectivist relativism in disguise. A moral judgment is not a feeling; it is not an act of the emotions, but an act of the intellect. We must insist on that.

Yet another manifestation of relativism is that moral discussion is increasingly considered offensive, as though to present an argument or even a fact relevant to judgment were to commit an act of aggression. Indeed, a student once screamed at me, not for expressing my view about partial-birth abortion, *but merely for explaining what it is.* Why did she scream? Partly, no doubt, because I had hit a nerve, but also because she didn't believe moral judgments are susceptible to argument; so screaming is all that is left. The screaming is self-justifying because it is taken as further confirmation of the fact that rational discourse about such matters is impossible.

Yet another manifestation of relativism is that university people misunderstand tolerance. Rightly understood, the virtue of tolerance *requires* moral judgment, because one must reason out which things are to be tolerated and which things are not. But university people think tolerance requires *suspending* moral judgment. This, of course, makes it impossible to practice the virtue of tolerance at all. We don't know how to distinguish between things which ought to be tolerated, like silly bumper stickers, and things that ought not be tolerated, like cheating on examinations. When we do make distinctions, we enforce them by arbitrary fiat, because, not having emerged from sound moral reasoning, they cannot stand rational examination. This is the origin of repressive campus speech codes and other forms of "political correctness." You would think that political correctness were a symptom of anything *but* moral relativism, because the practitioners of political correctness are so domatically self-righteous. But the reason that they can get away with being so dogmatic is precisely that the older traditions of moral discourse have almost vanished.

I see great confusion in the lives of my students, and a despair which comes from thinking that there are no answers. On the basis of what my students tell me, it seems that their lives are in greater moral disorder today than they were fifteen years ago. But I also see a good sign. The situation has now become so bad that unlike the students I taught fifteen years ago, they *recognize* the disorder in their lives and sometimes even admit it in the classroom. They bring it up themselves; they comment on the moral disorder of their parents' lives, and how this has paralyzed their own ability to make moral decisions. Our moral crisis has finally become so acute that people see that there is, in fact, a crisis.

This provides an opportunity for us to talk about the important things with them, but it is not easy to make use of it. Having passed through most of their formal education with no models of sound moral reasoning, students have no idea how to make a moral argument, or how to tell a good one from a poor one. Moreover, when today's student notices that he has made a moral judgment, he is likely to be ashamed of having done so. He feels the same remorse for making moral judgments that he ought to feel for violating the moral law. He is guilty of the crime of "judging."

Relativistic Fallacies

We need to consider certain common fallacies about relativism and its relatives. Merely for ease of reference and memory, I give each fallacy a name. The *seat-at-the-table fallacy* holds that relativism is an error, but an okay error. It's really good for us, the fallacy runs, because if everyone gets a seat at the table, then Christians get to sit down too. This assumption is naïve, because in reality, only those who do not rock the relativistic boat are allowed a seat at the table. The only Christians who are allowed to sit down are the Christians who deny their faith.

The *socialization fallacy* maintains that conscience is merely the residue of the way we were brought up. As Christians, we must disagree. To be sure, the outer edges of conscience can be modified by the way we are brought up, but the core is standard equipment. If this were not so, then why do you suppose that how children *are* brought up varies as little as it does? Do you know of any culture in which children are taught *not* to share, *not* to play fair, *not* to be honest? Can you think of one where they are taught to be cowards, and condemned for being brave? It isn't because we are taught the same rules that we know them; rather, it is because we all know the same rules that we teach them.

The *erosion fallacy* is that conscience is not built into us; it can erode and disappear. Many Christians accept this fallacy. They believe that the reason for the prevalence of relativism and other forms of moral skepticism is that the relativists and other moral skeptics have lost their conscience. If St. Paul is right about the law written on the heart, this diagnosis must be erroneous. The problem is not that people don't know the moral law, but that they tell themselves they don't. They have much better knowledge than they admit to themselves that they have. They wish to see things less clearly than they really do, usually so that they can do as they please.

The *many-moralities fallacy* asserts that moral beliefs are completely different in every culture. No, cultures differ about the details of morality, but not about the basics. To borrow another example from C. S. Lewis, cultures may disagree about whether a man may have one wife or four, but you will never find a culture that does not have the institution of marriage. Oftentimes people think that a culture does not recognize a particular moral rule just because, in that culture, people tend to wink at its violations. But there is a difference between taking a rule very seriously and not knowing it at all. Increasingly, the people of our society sleep with whomever they want to, and defend doing so. You would think they didn't know the wrong of sexual promiscuity. Yet they do know; very few of them will admit in mixed company just how many sexual partners they have had.

The *toleration fallacy* holds that tolerating people means suspending moral judgments. We can deal with this briefly because we have discussed true tolerance already. Tolerance cannot be practiced by suspending moral judgment. You must exercise moral judgment to recognize that tolerance is a virtue in the first place. You must make further moral judgments in order to know what should be tolerated and what should not.

We can deal with the *bad-behavior fallacy* more briefly still. This fallacy holds that if people violate the moral law, they must not know the moral law. On the contrary, the moral law is not unknown but merely inconvenient. We know what is right; we just don't do it. Many people express the bad-behavior fallacy, but few people will defend it when challenged.

The final fallacy is the *biblicist fallacy*, which holds that the knowledge of right and wrong comes only from the Bible. This fallacy is deadly, and I must speak about it at some length. When I condemn biblicism, please don't misunderstand me; I rely completely on the truth and authority of the Bible. But the biblicist fallacy is not biblical. Yes, God has made some things known only to the community of faith, but he has made some things known to humans generally. The Bible itself concurs. We learn from *conscience*, the law written on the heart, about which St. Paul speaks in Romans 2:14-15. We learn from our *design* (for example, the complementarity of the male and female and the incompleteness of one without the other). We learn from the *natural consequences* of our actions, built into the fabric of creation itself and affirmed in Galatians 6:7 (we reap what we sow); for example, it is in the nature of things that a father who deserts his children will have no one to stroke his brow when he is aged. We learn from a *Godward longing*, that obscure sense that taught even the pagans of Athens to seek for the "unknown god." And we learn from *the witness of creation itself*, for nothing brings itself into being, and the heavens proclaim the glory of God. The appendix of C. S. Lewis's *The Abolition of Man* provides a collection of extracts from philosophers and from moral and legal codes of the most diverse societies: aboriginal American, Hindu, Confucian, Taoist, ancient Egyptian, etc. The same ideas turn up everywhere: "You should not take your neighbor's wife"; "you should not lie and cheat"; "you should do unto others as you would have them do unto you"; and so forth.

A fascinating passage is found in Isaiah 28, which reads:

> Listen and hear my voice. Pay attention and hear what I say. When a farmer sows for planting, does he plow continually? Does he keep on breaking up and harrowing the soil? When he has leveled the surface, does he not sow caraway and scatter cumin? Does he not plant wheat in its place, barley in its plot and spelt in its field? His God instructs him and teaches him the right way.

That's an astonishing piece of writing, isn't it? The beginning of the passage contains nothing to surprise us. We know farmers know what to do. The astonishing thing about this that according to the end of the passage, he knows what to do *because God teaches him.* What could Isaiah possibly mean by that? What he means, I think, is that certain ways of farming, and more generally speaking, certain ways of living and of doing things, so to speak, go against the creational order. They rub against the grain. They don't prosper. Other ways do work out. They go with the grain; one thing leads easily to the next. We even begin to anticipate what will happen because we are gaining familiarity with the structures of creation: For the farmer, the nature of wheat and rye; for the husband, the nature of family and duty. This, too, is how God instructs us.

Let me return to the witness of our design. In Romans 1:26-27, Paul condemns homosexual acts and says that they are against "nature" (*physis*). This is one of the few times that the New Testament even uses the word "nature," and I think this was a very deliberate choice of term. Now "nature" can mean several things. In Galatians 2:15 when Paul speaks of those like himself who are Jews "by nature," he means those like himself who are Jews *by birth.* In Ephesians 2:3 when he says that when we lived according to our passions "we were by nature children of wrath," he means that when we lived according to our passions we were subject to wrath as a *natural consequence.* But our nature, considered simply, is our *design.* This sense of the term was familiar even to the pagan philosophers. We understand it as our *creational* design, as the pattern according to which God made us human beings. Homosexual acts are against our nature because they are contrary to that design— because men and women are complementary to each other, because they depend on each other for procreation and for becoming whole. By the way, when we speak of our nature as our design, we must understand that we are speaking not only of our physical design (important as that is), but of our emotional, intellectual, and spiritual design. The sexual powers were not designed for one-night stands. Women feel this with particular keenness. When I am speaking to a group about sexuality, I sometimes ask, "Women, what is it like to wake up the next morning and cry because he didn't call?" They all know what I am talking about.

Is biblical teaching the only way we know these things? No, and that is why the biblicist fallacy is mistaken. We know these things in all the ways that we have talked about, including conscience, Godward longing, and what happens when we try to live against the grain.

Regarding these things, the difference between believers and nonbelievers is *not* that we know them from the Bible and they don't know them at all, but that we know them by both biblical and extrabiblical means, and they know them only by the latter. This makes it harder for us than for them to pretend that we don't know what we really do know. We also know from the Bible the *solution* to the terrible problem that we don't live the way we know we ought to, for though extrabiblical knowledge includes some basic moral knowledge, it does not include the means of salvation.

Basics of Moral Apologetics

I take the basics of moral apologetics to be as follows. The first tenet is *dependence on God*. Only God can disarm the other party's hardness of heart. Success in responding to relativism (or for that matter in responding to people who admit that there is a moral law but who are confused about some part of it) does not come merely through the excellence of our technique, or through the completeness of our knowledge, however helpful these things may be. Not even our technique and knowledge will avail unless we cooperate with God, following His guidance, and praying before, during and after the encounter that the hearts of the people we are speaking with will be softened and their ears unplugged.

The second tenet of moral apologetics is *appraising the situation*. When confronted with moral confusions such as relativism, we must distinguish between honest intellectual difficulties, on the one hand, and evasions and self-deception, on the other. This is not easy to do. Most moral apologetics and most books about moral apologetics focus on the resolution of intellectual difficulties—that is, how to answer tough questions. The presupposition seems to be that most people have thought hard about morality, but run into logical puzzles that are beyond their capacity to solve. To be sure, this can happen. Much of the time, however, that's not what is going on at all. The person is merely putting up a smokescreen. Some smokescreens are easy to recognize, while others are difficult. That's why it is so important to appraise the situation. Honest intellectual difficulties require a certain kind of response, but smokescreens require another.

Here is an example of what I mean by an honest intellectual difficulty. Someone says, "I've been listening to what you say about God. But if God is good and all-powerful, then why is there suffering?" Now this is critical: He asks *because he wants to know the answer*. Not knowing bothers him. But now you must appraise the situation further. Why does it bother him? It may bother him philosophically—he is puzzled and wants to know. In this case, you give him a technical solution, the kind you can put on the blackboard: "Let's talk about free will." On the other hand, it may bother him emotionally—he is upset. Maybe his father is dying of cancer. Maybe girlfriend won't answer his calls. In this case you give him reassurance: "I can give you some technical solutions if you want; and I think so far as they go, they're pretty good. But I'll admit to you that I don't know the whole answer as to why God permits suffering. I *do* know how God views our suffering, though, because he took the worst of it upon Himself for us. That's what the Cross is all about. With that kind of a God, I can wait for the rest of the answer."

Now here is an example of what I mean by evasion or self-deception. Someone says the same thing as the other fellow: "I've been listening to what you say about God. But if God is good and all-powerful, then why is there suffering?" But he *doesn't* ask because he wants to know the answer; rather he is playing an intellectual game. Pontius Pilate was a questioner of this kind; he asked Jesus, "What is truth?"—not to begin a conversation, but to end it. Honest intellectual difficulties require solution; but evasions and self-deceptions require something quite different. The former need to be exposed; the latter need to be unmasked. You have to find a way to burst the bubble, to blow away the smokescreen. Sometimes the best answer is a sharp word, sometimes a sharp question, sometimes silence. Unmasking is a much more difficult apologetical art than providing solutions, and we have hardly begun to learn it.

Jesus, however, knew it well. Consider his conversation with the woman at the well. At first it seems that two different conversations are going on because she uses words as a game. But Jesus doesn't respond to her words. She demands to know why He asks *her* for water, because she is a Samaritan and He is a Jew. Instead of answering, He tells her that if she knew who was asking, she would ask *Him* for living water.

She asks where He expects to get this living water. Instead of answering, He tells her what it is like. Sarcastically, she demands it of Him. Instead of answering, He instructs her to call her husband, knowing that she has had five husbands and is living with a man to whom she is not married. She declares Him a prophet but tries to argue about where to worship. Instead of answering, He declares that an hour is coming that will make that quarrel obsolete. By the end of the conversation, her evasions are blown away, and she brings the whole village to hear Him.

Which do we meet more often in moral apologetics: Honest intellectual difficulty or smokescreens? It would very difficult to prove this sort of thing, but my experience in both in groups and one-to-one discussion leads me to believe that smokescreens are more common by far. When we fail to recognize them as smokescreens and suppose that they are honest intellectual difficulties, our fine intellectual responses merely allow the people with whom we are speaking opportunities to play further intellectual games. This does not advance the truth.

Suppose, however, that you recognize a smokescreen and succeed in blowing it away. What happens then? That depends largely on the level of education of the person with whom you are speaking because educated people are much quicker at devising smokescreens. An uneducated evader whose smokescreen is blown away may think "My golly, I've been lying to myself. Maybe I'd better stop blowing smoke, and just listen." But an educated evader sniffs the wind from afar, and by the time his smokescreen is blown away, he has three other smokepots ready to be brought online. You aren't talking with someone who wants to know the truth and is trying his best to find it. You are talking with someone who already knows part of the truth, suspects the rest, tells himself that he doesn't, and is trying to keep the conversation from reaching such a crisis that he will have to start being honest.

How can we talk with people who know or suspect the moral truth but who don't admit to themselves all they know? I will confine myself to the simplest of all gambits because once you get the idea, you will think of others. Often it helps just to *turn back the question*. A student once asked, "Isn't morality all just really relative? How do we even know that murder is wrong?" Now was this an honest intellectual difficulty or a smokescreen? I recognized at once that it was a smokescreen. Never believe anyone who claims ignorance of a basic moral rule like "Do not murder." The problem was self-deception. So I responded, "Are you in any doubt about murder being wrong?" My student did not expect that reply. No doubt he had asked his question before—in class or in dormitory conversations—and had received nothing but praise and approving glances. "Perceptive lad. He'll go far." He wasn't at all prepared to be asked, "Do you mean it?" Stumbling a bit, he replied, "Some people might say that murder was all right." I pressed, "Yes, but I'm not asking some people. I'm asking you. Have you any real doubt about murder being wrong for everybody?" Confronted in this way, he broke down and admitted, "No, I guess not." That gave me the opening to say, "Then we don't have to waste time on things you aren't really in doubt about, like whether morality is relative. Tell me something that you *are* in doubt about." Now this was a moment of truth for this student. Was he suddenly cured of all moral confusion? Certainly not, but he had learned something—even if only about himself. He had learned that he wasn't as ignorant as he wanted to believe that he was.

You see, even the relativist knows deep down that relativism is false. The task of the moral apologist is only ten percent teaching; the other ninety percent is uncovering. He labors not to fill the empty conscience, but to dredge the sunken conscience—to bring people face to face with what they really know, but suppress. The Adversary will try to keep it down, but by the grace of God we can sometimes help bring it to the surface. That is our goal.

Chapter Six

—⟨≈⟩—

PRACTICAL RESPONSES TO
RELATIVISM AND POSTMODERNISM:
PART II?

WITH AUDIENCE DISCUSSION[1]

J. Budziszewski

J. Budziszewski (Ph.D., Yale) teaches government and philosophy at the University of Texas at Austin. Besides writing numerous journal articles, he has written half a dozen books including including Written on the Heart: The Case for Natural Law (InterVarsity) and The Revenge of Conscience: Politics and the Fall of Man (Spence). His newest book is The Beginning of Wisdom (Spence).

Abstract

"Now suppose someone honestly replies: 'No, I guess I really don't want to hear the answers.' You can say, 'All right. I'm not trying to embarrass you, but I'd like to know something: You must have had some motive for asking the questions. If it wasn't to know the answers, what was it?' This question makes people uncomfortable, but you need to ask it anyway. Why? Because in apologetics, we are often dealing directly with issues of the will—not just the intellect. Confusion of the mind interacts with obstinacy of the heart."

Specific Moral Questions

Q1: You discussed the student who espoused relativism and asked how we even know murder is wrong for everyone. Don't we doubt a lot of things for argument's sake (or hypothetically)?

A: Hypotheticals are useful, but I don't think the student was posing a hypothetical. I don't think he was asking, "*What if* someone were to say that murder were okay? How might we answer him?" Rather I think he was asking, "*Isn't* murder okay for those who say it is? *Can* you prove it isn't?" He wasn't asking how to answer a relativist; he was asserting that relativism is true. Of course, if I am mistaken about that, then I gave him the wrong answer.

By the way, we have to be extremely careful when we employ hypotheticals. We must try to make them *concrete and realistic.* There is a view in ethics called utilitarianism. Utilitarians believe that the right thing to do in every circumstance is whatever maximizes the sum total of pleasure—as though all pains and pleasures were put into a common pot. Philosopher Robert Nozick criticizes this crass philosophy by asking us to imagine an extraterrestrial intelligence who derives pleasure from eating human babies—so much pleasure that it outweighs all the pains of all the babies and all their parents. He asks, "Would that make it right for him to eat the babies?" Of course nothing could make it right to eat babies, but Nozick's scenario is less convincing to most people than you would expect; the counterfactual elements distract and confuse people. I oppose utilitarianism too, but I think we will be more convincing—and have an easier time avoiding error—if we imagine hypotheticals that we know could really happen. For example, a rapist might claim a utilitarian justification for his method of raping because he drugs the woman before raping her. This, he says, makes his pleasure greater than her pain; so the aggregate pleasure of society is increased. People find it easier to see what is wrong with utilitarian reasoning in a scenario like this than in a scenario like Nozick's because there aren't any science-fiction elements to confuse us. We don't have experience with extraterrestrial baby-eaters, but we do have experience with rapists who drug their victims.[2]

Q2: One topic on which there seems to be no room for debate is homosexuality. How do you deal with that?

A: I don't agree that there is no room for rational discussion. Most people absorb opinions about homosexuality without carefully thinking about them. Just get them to think about them! Many people are surprised to discover that arguments can be offered about such a subject at all; they think opinions about sex express mere preferences rather than reasoned conclusions. If you do present them with an argument about sex, they are so startled that they might actually consider it. Suppose someone says, "I'm uncomfortable with the idea of homosexual marriage, but I don't think we should discriminate." You can reply, "I see your point about discrimination. Discrimination certainly would be unjust *if* nothing were morally wrong with homosexual marriage. But that begs the question about whether anything is wrong with it; so let's talk about whether or not it is." Then you can talk about other things like the complementarity of the male and female—the way we "match," not merely physically but intellectually and emotionally. The male provides something to the female that she can't provide for herself; the female provides something for the male that he can't provide for himself; and both male and female provide different things to their children. A child needs both a Mom and a Dad. Try it. Provide the argument, and just see what happens. Even if you don't convince the other party, you'll change the climate of discussion because the other party will be thinking "My goodness! I didn't even know that reasons *could* be given about things like this." This plants seeds.

Be aware of the limits of different kinds of arguments. Some arguments are more effective—precisely because they are less complete—than others. Consider the argument that homosexual behavior has bad consequences, such as physiological damage and the spread of infectious disease. That's a pretty good argument, as far as it goes. The built-in consequences of our behavior are one of God's methods of instruction. The problem is that the argument doesn't go far enough. Our culture has the unfortunate idea that whenever you're confronted with one of the built-in bad consequences of your behavior, you should simply hotwire human nature to eliminate the bad consequence. Worried about disease? Use a condom. Suffering from physiological damage? Get the doctor to sew it up. Already infected? Demand a cure. What we ought to ask is how something which causes such consequences can be "loving" *even if there is* a way to fix the damage afterward.

Q3: You're presuming that there will never be a perfect barrier or protective method—that the methods don't work, and that we have lots of sick people to prove it.

A: I do think there will never be a perfect barrier or protective method. *Something* bad will always happen when we act contrary to our design: If not one thing, then another. If not physiological damage, for example, then emotional damage. But because people don't want to believe that, you have to take the next step. You have to raise consciousness about the fact that these bad consequences aren't merely something that *happens* to occur. They occur because the behavior is contrary to our *design*—to the way that we have been made. *That's why* no foolproof "protection" will be developed—but it's also why the behavior would be wrong *even if foolproof "protection" were developed.* Respect for the design reflects respect for the Designer; everyone feels the force of that reflection, whether or not you call attention to it. Notice, too, that awareness of the Designer opens up the conversation. People want to know about Him. So you can talk about that too. And that's even better because however important it is not to have illicit sex, we aren't reconciled with God just by not having it.

Morality, Motives, and Self-Deception

Q4: I teach biblical studies and contemporary issues at a secular college. What I have failed to understand all these years is that when I am logically presenting a philosophical, scientific, or biological argument—say, about abortion or homosexuality—the students just don't get it. I think I've been appraising the situation wrongly. I've been thinking that if intellectually they should take my side, but they don't, then for some reason they must be having intellectual difficulty. Perhaps it's not that at all. Could it be the self-deception you're talking about?

A: Yes, that's right: Self-deception certainly can prevent a person from recognizing the force of a logical argument. This doesn't mean that there isn't any hope of breaking through. If we depend on God's grace, certain techniques of argument can sometimes break through, and I'll take time to talk about them as we go along. However, the technique of breaking through self-deception goes beyond merely presenting a better logical argument. You use one method to crack open the shutters of self-deception; when they open, that's when you offer your argument. You can't use the argument in order to crack open the shutters; they have to be cracked open before the other party will listen to the argument at all. When you do offer your argument, by the way, you may have to reason quickly because the shutters may be open for only a moment or two.

Q5: We were in a role-playing situation in a college reading group that I'm in, and I was startled by the response of one of the people. One guy spouted off, "How do we know that murder is wrong?" A female student immediately responded: "You see that lady over there in the wheelchair? Come on. Let's go hack her to death." What about going to an extreme with your example? Is there danger in that?

A: Yes, there is risk—but sometimes the risk is acceptable. Occasionally I make strong remarks of that sort. Sometimes you will be mistaken *not* to speak strongly; sometimes you will be mistaken if you do. If you humbly pay heed to your mistakes, you will develop discernment. By the way, anger from the other party is not necessarily evidence that you have erred. Of course you should never be insulting or *try* to arouse anger, but an angry response is not necessarily bad. It can even provide you with an opportunity. Suppose the other fellow says, "How dare you say something like that? What kind of person do you think I am?" You can reply, "Slow down. There is nothing in what *I've* said to make you angry; I'm merely calling attention to the implications of your position. Is there something in *you* to make you angry?" Perhaps the other party says, "You're trying to make me out as the kind of person who would hack a lady in a wheelchair to death." Then you can say, "I'm not trying to make you out as any sort of person. But if there really were nothing wrong with murder, then wouldn't it be all right to be that sort of person? Why, in that case, should you mind being made out as one?" Or perhaps he says, "You're making an emotional argument—a cheap appeal to sympathy for helpless people." Then you can say, "Good moral judgment doesn't lie in *not having* emotions. The idea is to have the right emotions, in the right way, at the right times, toward the right persons, for the right reasons. In the case of murder, I think the emotion of sympathy for the victim is one of the right ones. Don't you?" Of course, gut reactions don't by themselves reveal the rightness or wrongness of something, *but they are included in the relevant data that ought to be considered.* So I don't think we have to be afraid of them either.

Before we continue, let me mention another strategy for breaking through self-deception: *Dissipating smoke.* While this approach can be effective in evangelism, it can also be useful in moral apologetics too. Sometimes a person will fire one objection after another at you. Even though you reply to each objection, he seems unfazed and goes on to ask another one—perhaps even on a completely unrelated subject. If this goes on long enough and you don't seem to be getting anywhere, you should begin wondering whether the person truly wants to get somewhere. Perhaps he only thinks he does.

Of course it may be that every one of these dozens of questions represents a serious intellectual problem for him. If so, then every one requires a serious intellectual answer. But it may also be that these dozens of questions are a smokescreen that he uses to keep the conversation from reaching his real issues, whatever they may be. How can you find out which is the case? How can you test the waters? One way is to ask something like this:

> You've got lots of questions. I've only answered a few of them, and I see that you have many more. Let me take a moment to ask you a question. Suppose we shut ourselves in a room for a few weeks, had our food delivered, and used every waking hour to talk. Suppose you asked every last one of your questions, and I answered each one to your own intellectual satisfaction. *Would you then change your mind?*

You may be surprised how many people answer *No.* If a person does say *No*, turn his answer back on him: "If you wouldn't be convinced even if I gave responses that you found completely satisfactory to each one of your objections, *then these objections must not be the reason you don't believe.* What do you think *is* the real reason?" You see, you have blown away his smokescreen. I don't say that he will instantly be converted. But he will have discovered his smokescreen for what it is.

Q6: I once did have a student who machine-gunned questions. I'd answer one, and then he'd switch to a different topic. Finally I said, "Do you really want these questions answered? Because if you don't, you're just wasting my time and yours. Is this something you're really interested in or just something to do this half hour?" He said, "No, I really want to." And then the conversation did shift to one specific topic and was more focused.

A: That was a good conversational move. Sometimes, though, a person may give an *insincere* answer to a question like the one you asked. He replies, "No, I really want to," not because he really does want to, but because it would be a loss of face to admit that he really doesn't. The reason I take the *would you be convinced* approach is that it doesn't seem to threaten the same loss of face.

Now suppose someone honestly replies: "No, I guess I really don't want to hear the answers." You can say, "All right. I'm not trying to embarrass you, but I'd like to know something: You must have had some motive for asking the questions. If it wasn't to know the answers, what was it?" This question makes people uncomfortable, but you need to ask it anyway. Why? Because in apologetics, we are often dealing directly with issues of the will—not just the intellect. Confusion of the mind interacts with obstinacy of the heart.

Shall we talk about some other strategies for breaking through self-deception? One such strategy is *connecting the dots*. The anecdote I am about to tell was related to me by a friend, who at the time of the story was the chaplain to a Christian student group at a public university. A young women in the group sought him out for counseling. From the outside, you wouldn't have known she had a problem. She was attractive, self-possessed, confident, cheerful, outgoing—a campus leader. She had recently thrown herself into pro-abortion activities, marching in a pro-abortion parade on campus, giving a speech to her rhetoric class on how her abortion had solved all her personal problems, and so forth.

Unbeknownst to anyone but my friend, she was suffering from suicidal depression. Trying to get to the bottom of it, he asked a question. He said, "If you hadn't had your own abortion, about when would the baby have been born?"

She thought about it and she said, "About now."

And he said, "And how long have you been suffering this depression?"

Again she said, "About now." It was time for the dead baby to be born, and her depression was at its peak. He didn't have to say, "Do you see a connection here?" She saw the connection herself; she connected the dots. This sort of thing is common. People *don't want* to connect certain dots. They try hard *not* to connect them. Sometimes they've already connected them subconsciously, but don't want to admit it to themselves. Sometimes they suspect that there is a dot to be connected here, but they just won't look at that part of the picture. If you ask the right questions, you can help them.

Still another strategy is *releasing the catch*. This story too comes from the annals of abortion counseling. Consider: You can't not know that it is wrong to deliberately take innocent human life; this, surely, is one of the laws "written on the heart." Regarding abortion, it's difficult not to recognize that the unborn child is innocent and human. And in this age of sonograms, it's difficult not to recognize that the baby is alive. So you can count on the fact that women who have aborted their babies are bearing the burden of suppressed guilt that will surface somehow. But some women refuse to acknowledge or discuss this burden unless someone *releases the catch* on the box of their locked-up thoughts and feelings. They need—so to speak—permission to talk. Let me illustrate.

My wife, Sandra, is one of the most gifted crisis pregnancy counselors I've ever met. Women who seek counsel at crisis pregnancy centers routinely answer certain questions on "intake" forms. My wife always goes over the form with them afterward, asking the same questions verbally. "Have you had any previous abortions?" And many have. The next question is "Afterward, did you experience any physical or emotional side effects?" This time the almost inevitable answer is "No." But the woman isn't really thinking "No"; she is only telling herself "No." So my wife pauses for a moment before going on. And in that pause, things happen.

Perhaps the woman adds, ". . . other than the usual." Then Sandra can ask, "What's the usual?" Or perhaps the woman adds, ". . . but I'd never do it again." And then Sandra can ask, "Why wouldn't you do it again?" The pause is completely non-directive—yet all of a sudden the conversation changes direction, *just because the woman has been given permission to say something.* That's releasing the catch.

I suspect the standard methods of psychological survey research won't catch up with the experience of Christian counselors here for another generation or two. Let's say you're investigating the question of whether there is such a thing as post-abortion trauma, and you ask women whether they have suffered it. The culture does not permit them to say, "Yes, I've suffered terribly." So they reply in the negative. The problem is that the question doesn't include provision for a pause.

Releasing the catch is non-directive. As we saw a few minutes ago, there are occasions in moral apologetics when you have to be more confrontational. When is it right to confront, and when isn't it? For this you need discernment. It is possible to make a mistake in either direction: To be confrontational when you ought to be non-directive, and to be non-directive when you ought to confront. I think it's also partly a matter of personal gift. Some people are better equipped by God to deal with one sort of situation, and if they are willing to respond to God, He may begin bringing such situations to them. Others are better equipped to deal with another sort of situation, and God may bring that kind to them. But we have to keep a sharp eye on ourselves to make sure that our preference is not out of kilter with the needs of the situation—to make sure, for example, that we aren't interpreting every situation as the kind that calls for gentle confrontation just because we happen to be good at it.

Here is a mildly confrontational technique: *Playing back the tape.* Perhaps a student, a professor, a friend raises a lot of questions — but each time, with mathematical precision, he interrupts with another question just as you are about to complete the answer. That ought to make you suspicious. On one such occasion, I asked my questioner, "Do you notice what you've been doing here? You've asked a lot of questions, and that's fine. But each time you've interrupted my answer just as I was about to reach the punch-line." Rather than becoming defensive, the fellow said, "Yeah, I guess I do," adding "Why do you think I do that?" Instead of answering I asked "Why do *you* think you do that?" He said, "I guess I must not want to hear your answers." I replied, "Then the important question is why you don't want to hear them. Can we talk about that instead?" He agreed, and there was a change in the direction of the conversation. That's what I mean by playing back the tape.

Another approach to note is *calling attention to the obvious.* There are some things that people plainly know, but persist in overlooking. My wife tells me that some women say to her, "I just can't have a baby right now." The presupposition of such a remark is that the woman doesn't yet have a baby. My wife—non-directively, as before—asks, "Well, what do you call what's inside you?" Most women (except for the few who have been thoroughly drilled in feminist apologetics and rhetoric) reply, "I call it a baby." That gives Sandra permission to say, "In that case, it seems that the question before you isn't whether you can have a baby right now, but what to do with the one you've already got."

Do you see how this works? No new information is added beyond what the woman already knows. She spontaneously answers, "I call it a baby"; its babyhood is obvious to her. You don't have to engage in apologetics and say, "Let's talk about whether what you're carrying is human life." She knows she is. You are merely helping her to *notice* what she knows by asking a few questions in a disarming manner.

Postmodernism, Truth, and the "Creation of Reality"

Q7: What I think you're describing is the importance of definition. One recent author has suggested that in whatever context we happen to be, we ought to ask: "Whose definition is that, and what purposes are served by it?" We need to understand that there's a reason, a purpose, for that kind of definition.

A: Sometimes that is an appropriate question, but we have to be careful. When asked the wrong way, it turns us off course. Postmodernists don't believe in truth. They think all propositions are mere projections of someone's interests. In their view, the only question worth asking about a proposition is whose interests it projects. But we think there is another issue: Is the proposition *true?* So, although we do sometimes need to ask whether a person believes a proposition only because it serves his interests, we should avoid asking this question in the way that postmodernists do—in a way that distracts us from the truth issue. Rather, we should ask it in the way that befits a Christian—in a way that *returns* us to the truth issue.

Q8: My question is similar. A colleague of mine is a constructionist in the field of psychology; she believes reality is just a social construction. When I raise the question of realism vs. constructivism, her defense is: "Those are the radical constructionists. I'm not a radical." She claims that we are very close in viewpoint, which confuses me since we differ fundamentally. I think her position boils down to what you said earlier about moral vs. epistemological relativism: She denies she's a relativist in epistemology but holds to a relativism in morality. I keep saying you can't really dichotomize.

A: Social constructionism is the idea that reality isn't out there waiting to be perceived, discovered, recognized—but that we create it ourselves. What makes this error superficially plausible is that it contains a grain of truth; the social constructionist views that grain with carnival mirrors and sees an entire wheat field. Here is the grain of truth: In a certain limited sense, we really do "construct" *some* features of our social reality. To take a trivially obvious example, it *really is* true that because we have agreed among ourselves that it shall be so, we shouldn't drive on the left side of the road in the United States. And it *really is* true that because English drivers have agreed among themselves that it shall be so, they *should* drive on the left side of the road in England. So there are some cases where social agreement or convention—if you like (though I don't), "construction"—can make something true that wouldn't be true otherwise.

The problem with social constructionism is that these conventions merely "fill in the blanks" in a moral structure which is already mostly given. Social agreement can make it wrong to drive on the left side of the road, but it can do this *only because it is already wrong to endanger our neighbors,* and the agreement merely determines which of several ways we will choose to avoid endangering them. If we so decide, we can make it wrong to drive on the right instead of wrong to drive on the left—but no decision can ever make it right to endanger our neighbors.

Even past theories of objective morality acknowledged that social conventions "fill in the blanks" of a reality already mostly given. Thomas Aquinas, the greatest of natural law thinkers, called this the "determination of certain generalities." He didn't see it as "creating moral reality" but as choosing between different ways of fulfilling moral reality.

Unfortunately, social constructivists fail to distinguish social conventions that we can construct from the great moral givens that we cannot construct. So what you need to do here is emphasize the distinction. We construct driving regulations, but we do not construct the underlying norm of respect for our neighbors on the road. We construct suitable punishments for crimes, but we do not construct the underlying norm that crimes should be requited by suitable punishments. If you need to, use extreme examples. Is it just a social construction that the Nazis were wrong to stuff Jews into gas chambers? The Nazis had made a different agreement among themselves. Did that make it right to kill Jews "for them"?

Waiting for an Opportunity

Let me mention just one more strategy for breaking through the shutters of obstinacy and self-deception. Strictly speaking, it isn't a "strategy" at all, because it is simply *waiting for an opportunity from God.* You see, God has his own apologetics, which escape all of our plans, techniques, and calculations.

At the beginning of every semester, when I explain to my students about the course and how I teach it, I say something like this:

> Every teacher approaches his material from some perspective—tacit or explicit—and I think you have a right to know where I'm coming from. If I were a Marxist, feminist, or postmodernist, I'd tell you that I was a Marxist, feminist, or postmodernist. I'm not any of those things; I am a Christian. Jesus Christ and His teachings are crucial to my outlook on the world and everything in it. I try to present every view fairly, and I won't beat you over the head with my own; in fact I encourage you to express your own views on the course material, provided that you give reasoned arguments for them. Make good use of this information. If anything that I say is unreasonable or distorted, you now have a fighting chance of finding out.

One semester I forgot to explain about my faith. I explained every other necessary thing about the course and about myself, but I didn't mention that I was a Christian. After returning to my office, I realized my mistake and thought, "That was stupid." And this time it turned out for the good.

For several weeks into the course, I taught about nothing but Aristotle's ethics. I hadn't said anything which would "sound Christian." One day during office hours, a young man in the course—a student in his thirties—showed up at the door and said, "Professor, I've gotta' talk to you."

I told him to come in and asked, "What do we gotta' talk about?"

He said, "I gotta' tell you that I'm getting scared."

"Why are you getting scared?"

"Because you're scaring me. See? I'm shaking." He was a melodramatic sort of guy, and he held out his shaking hand to prove it.

I inquired, "How am I scaring you?"

He said, "It isn't you. It's Aristotle."

I said, "How is Aristotle scaring you?"

Finally he got to the point: "In this book of his, he keeps talking about virtue, and it's made me realize I haven't lived a virtuous life."

I had not created this opportunity. There had not been any technique. I hadn't practiced turning back the question, dissipating smoke, connecting the dots—any of those things. In all the days I had lectured about Aristotle, I had never once mentioned words like *God, sin, judgment,* or even *moral law.* Yet the Holy Spirit had used the writing of a pagan philosopher to produce conviction of sin in the heart of this young man.

God was present, and we have to remember who is Sovereign in this business.

---

[1] For the sake of clarity, some of the questions were rephrased, and some of the answers were revised.

[2] The science-fiction sort of hypothetical poses other dangers too. For instance, in order to settle a question about the philosophy of personal identity, a philosopher might ask, "Suppose if you are using a 'transporter' as in the *Star Trek* stories, but the teleportation machine malfunctions. You rematerialize in the new location—but you don't dematerialize in the old location. Which one is really you? Or are both of them really you?" By arguing about the scenario a person may think he is gaining new insight, but in fact the scenario merely begs the question. For if the question under debate is the nature of human identity, why should I even agree that a human being *could* be "transported" in the *Star Trek* fashion—that he *could* be taken apart into molecules, "beamed" across space, reassembled, and still be himself? The supposition seems to be that human identity can be reduced to an arrangement of matter, but that is just what we ought to be debating.

Chapter Seven

CAN A GOOD GOD ALLOW EVIL AND SUFFERING?

R. Douglas Geivett

Dr. R. Douglas Geivett is professor of philosophy and director of the Talbot Department of Philosophy at Biola University. He is the author of Evil and the Evidence for God, co-editor of In Defense of Miracles and Contemporary Perspectives on Religious Epistemology, and contributor to numerous books.

Abstract

"Some time ago I debated the question, 'Does God exist?' with an agnostic philosopher and friend of mine. During the question-and-answer session afterward, one woman approached the microphone and with obvious rage began to explain why her experience with pain and suffering prevented her from believing that God exists. It was as if she blamed me for this because I believed in God. As tactfully as I could, I said to her, 'I can't help but notice that you seem very angry. But with whom are you angry, if God does not exist? Are you angry with me for believing in God? How does that help you? The real question is: "Are you sure you don't believe in God?" Perhaps it isn't that you don't believe in God, but that you're angry with God. But consider what God has done for you through Jesus Christ. Can you really resent a God like that?'"

Oᴜʀ ᴛᴏᴘɪᴄ, ᴛʜᴇ ᴘʀᴏʙʟᴇᴍ ᴏғ ᴇᴠɪʟ, concerns us all. It is a problem we all encounter in our disciplines and in our personal lives. We meet people, both inside and outside the academy, who stumble over this obstacle to faith. We may be used by God to help them sort through this aspect of their spiritual pilgrimage. Of course, each of us will at times find our own faith disturbed by the reality of evil in the world. I believe that our spiritual and intellectual lives go hand in hand. My spirituality is affected by my scholarship, and my scholarship is affected by the state of my soul. Nowhere is this interplay more significant than in my reflections upon the justice of God's permission of horrendous evils.

Evil and Suffering Are Universal

It certainly is not difficult to identify examples of concrete evils that provoke us to wonder: "*Why is there evil in the world?*" The enigma of evil is a prominent theme in great literature. Though it portrays imaginary worlds, it is a powerful tool for expressing the realities and nuances of human experience. Consider Victor Hugo's depiction of human suffering in the following passage from *Les Misérables*:

> Man overboard! Who cares? The ship sails on. The wind is up, the dark ship must keep to its destined course. It passes on . . . . he hollers, stretches out his hands. They do not hear him . . . .What a specter is that disappearing sail! He watches it, follows it frantically. It moves away, grows dim, diminishes. He was just there, one of the crew . . . . Now, what has become of him? He slipped. He fell. It's all over! He is in the monstrous deep. . . . the voracious ocean is eager to devour him. The monster plays with his agony. It is all liquid hatred to him. He tries to defend, to sustain himself; he struggles; he swims. . . . There are birds in

the clouds, even as there are angels above human distresses, but what can they do for him? They sing, fly, and soar, while he gasps. . . . Men are gone. Where is God? He screams, "Help! Someone! Help!" He screams over and over. Nothing on the horizon. Nothing in the sky. He implores the lofty sky, the endless waves, the reefs; all are deaf. He begs the storms; but impassive, they obey only the infinite. . . . What can he do? He yields to despair. Worn out, he seeks death, no longer resists, gives up, lets go, tumbles into the mournful depths of the abyss forever. . . . The soul drifting in that sea may become a corpse. Who shall restore it to life?[1]

Is this not poignant? How does Hugo describe in such psychologically rich detail an experience that he himself has not had? Clearly, it is not autobiographical, as the man in the story does not live to describe the experience. How then does the novelist translate his character's inner world with such uncanny depth of insight? His tale is a symbolic representation of the many different ways in which men and women experience loss, disappointment, disillusionment, frustration, silence, and alienation from God.

Hugo's drowning man initially cries out, hoping against hope for some assistance. He first calls out to his shipmates. But they do not hear him. He then casts about for some other source of salvation. The birds fly overhead, yet they are powerless and oblivious. Their carefree spirit is an insult to his deplorable condition. What about the elements themselves that engulf him? Is salvation to be had there? No, they are the immediate *problem*. And God—where is God? Might He yet deliver? Time goes by. The man swims and treads water, conserving his strength as much as possible, and God does nothing to intervene. And so the man's thoughts turn from the hopeless prospect of survival to the possibility that, when he dies, all will not be lost. He may yet be raised.

What powerful images Hugo offers—of ways that humans cling to anything that would give them hope, even as the world falls apart around them. I might have chosen an example of suffering or evil from the front page of any newspaper, or told of my own griefs or of those close to me. But isn't it also revealing to have a passage from literature that speaks of an experience foreign to all of us, which nonetheless parallels things we do know experientially.

The Spectacle of Misery

Let us consider another masterful depiction of suffering in literature—one that is, I believe, an account of actual historical events. The biblical narrative of Job recounts the trials that intruded, by divine permission, into the life of a righteous man. God instructed Satan: "Everything he has is in your hands, but on the man himself do not lay a finger" (Job 1:12).[2] And so Satan did everything in his power to induce despair and dissolve faith. In a single day, the wealthy Job was reduced to utter destitution and informed that all his sons and daughters had died in a natural disaster. In the words of Puritan author, Thomas Watson, "Job was a spectacle of misery."[3] His wife, an exasperated victim of all of these events as well, counseled her husband with these querulous words: "Curse God and die!" (Job 2:9).

I have often wondered about the significance of that statement. What thoughts and feelings did she mean to express? One possibility is that her desperation had convinced her that cursing God was the only thing now that made sense, that this was the most natural and appropriate, even the inevitable, response to the siphoning of all that was significant in her life. Surely she realized the terrible consequences of literally cursing God: anyone who does that is treading on thin ice and had better be prepared to die. But does she care? In light of her losses, God does not seem to care a great deal. So what if cursing God leads to punishment by death? Job's better half no longer believed God was worthy of her trust. Thus, it was immaterial whether God would punish her resentment by killing her. He had utterly failed to earn her respect. This anguished interpretation may be summarized in this way: "In light of our wretched circumstances and God's betrayal, we may as well die."

An alternative interpretation of her peevish declamation highlights the consequences of abandoning faith: "If you curse God and turn your back on Him, acting as if there is no God (which is in part what it would signify to curse God), then you might as well die. For who can live without God?"

Both interpretations illustrate attitudes that individuals sometimes adopt as they think about evil and its theological implications. And that is our theme here: *What is the religious significance of evil and suffering in the world?*

Evil Is Both an Intellectual and an Existential Problem

I'm often invited to address the problem of evil from one of two distinct perspectives. At times I'm asked to speak about the intellectual obstacle that evil presents to religious conviction. Even when this *intellectual* problem of evil is the focus of my message, I always assume what is generally the case: that there are those in the audience for whom intellectual doubts are not the major concern. Usually there is someone present who is threatened with disillusionment by some overwhelming circumstance, some deep disappointment, some instance of pain, evil, or suffering. It is very little help to those who are actively suffering to address the concerns of the intellect and offer a solution to some *philosophical* problem of evil. And yet—with some trepidation—I want to suggest that even in the abstract theoretical realm of philosophical discussion there may be something of substance for the weary sufferer that would reach her even in her hour of pain.

On other occasions, I'm invited to speak on the role of adversity in spiritual formation. At such times, I recognize there are those in the audience who struggle mightily with the intellectual dimensions of the problem of evil. They are most eager to find a solution to the logical and evidential problems in order to get on with believing in God. In these circumstances, my chief concern—to make sense of how evil actually plays a constructive role in our spiritual development and in fostering confidence in God—may not speak to the intellectual needs of some in the audience.

The problem of evil then has two important dimensions—the intellectual-apologetic and the existential-pastoral. These dimensions of concern seem, on the surface, to be entirely unrelated. And yet, I believe, they are actually complementary because of the intimate connection between our spiritual and our intellectual formation.

There are three distinct types of arguments from evil that sabotage conviction that God exists or that God is worthy of our affection. The first two arguments are primarily *intellectual* in nature. The third is more broadly *spiritual* and *existential.* While the first two are philosophical, they are not so narrowly philosophical that non-philosophers cannot be moved by them. The third is more personal and pastoral. And yet even the most rigorously intellectual of sufferers requires a pastoral response. In this chapter we shall focus only on the intellectual or philosophical challenge of evil.

The Master Interrogator

Before examining two philosophical arguments in detail, let me recommend a methodology that is very useful when commending the Christian worldview, and particularly when we are confronted with the problem of evil as an objection to Christianity. This methodology is most helpful when an objection is tersely and emphatically asserted against the faith of Christians. It is the strategy, illustrated so masterfully by Jesus Christ, of parrying a question with a question.

In the Gospel of Mark 2:1:3-6, we find a description of five different encounters between Jesus and the intelligentsia of his day—the scribes, Pharisees, and Sadducees. This entourage confronted him at various times with serious challenges to the credibility of his claims. His characteristic response was to answer a question with a question. Understand, however, that this was not a dodge. It was quite purposeful and rhetorically powerful. In the fifth episode (3:1-6) at the apex of Jesus' confrontations with Israel's religious leaders, a group of Pharisees and Sadducees were his key adversaries. They were the preeminent scholars of their generation and the chief intellectual representatives of the Hebraic tradition— the "Bible answer men" for their time. They had long been at odds with Jesus, and the tension had steadily mounted to a shrill crescendo. By this time the leaders themselves had learned from painful and embarrassing experience that it was a mistake to interrogate Jesus directly. He always managed to frustrate his inquisitors with even more fundamental questions than theirs, questions that revealed their obtuse hearts and malevolent intentions. His method exposed indefensible assumptions behind their questions.

So imagine their experiment with an alternative approach when these religious leaders noticed a man with a withered hand, loitering in a conspicuous location within the synagogue on the Sabbath. Reasoning that Jesus would soon arrive, they felt sure, based on past experience, that Jesus would see the man, take pity on him, and heal him. This would present them with a momentous opportunity, with limited personal risk to themselves. They would step forth from the shadows and charge Jesus with doing work on the Sabbath, a violation of the will of God and hence a sin, according to their understanding. Thus, Jesus would be disqualified as a pretended messenger from God.

Sure enough, just as they had expected, Jesus entered the synagogue, immediately spotted the man with a deformity, and called him over. The religious leaders, now huddled in a corner casting glances over their shoulders to monitor the progress of their plan, must have congratulated themselves on their ingenuity. Jesus was acting precisely as predicted. What glee! But then something went wrong. For some reason, Jesus was speaking directly to them!

Let us imagine the interchange:

Jesus: "Gentleman, I have a question for you."

Sadducee #1: "For *us*? You're talking to us? Hey (in the direction of Sadducee #2), I think he's looking at *you*."

Sadducee #2: "Oh . . . ."

Jesus, again: "Gentlemen, I have a question for you."

After much swallowing and futile ducking behind the fellow next to him, a Pharisee speaks up rather weakly: "Yes, what's the question?"

Jesus: "Well, as you know, today's the Sabbath. Perhaps you've noticed there's a man here with a withered hand. My heart goes out to him. Surely yours must, too. Now, I could do something about it; I could heal him. But today is the Sabbath. Now here's my question: What should I do in this situation? You're the experts in these matters. Is it lawful to *kill* or to *do good* on the Sabbath? Can you help me with this dilemma?"

Jesus asks a penetrating question. Initially the question sounds a bit bizarre and out of place. But, looking intently in their direction, Jesus waits for a response. And the Bible says that they remained silent. This is a good indication that they had learned quite a lot from their past encounters with Jesus. They kept silent. Perhaps they made excuses for not answering his question directly.

How is the awkward silence broken? A senior member of the group, feeling awkward with the silence, finally croaks: "I've got laryngitis. Someone else will have to handle this one."

Another volunteers helpfully: "Wait a minute. Didn't Jesse, here, write his dissertation on this?"

No. The intelligentsia remained silent. The passage recounts that Jesus looked at them in anger. Again they had been cornered by their own machinations. Again their tactics had backfired. But then, remarkably, Jesus seemed to walk unwittingly right into their trap. He turned to the disabled man and instructed him, "Stretch out your hand." When the man complied, his hand was healed. The religious authorities immediately left and reconvened in a secret location. There they plotted to destroy Jesus. (Imagine muffled conversation in a back room somewhere, with cigars burning.) Whether it ever occurred to them or not, the reader of Mark's Gospel cannot fail to notice the uncanny aptness of the earlier words of Jesus—he who knew their hearts and their ultimate intentions—when he asked: "Is it lawful to kill or to do good?"

We learn from this glimpse of Jesus in action that he frequently parried a question or a challenge with a question of his own. When he brought his accusers' assumptions into the light, they often retreated into silent consternation to await a fresh opportunity after further preparation. What is the lesson for us who would commend the faith to our peers?

When we commend the Christian worldview to others, with optimism and joy, sooner or later we will encounter objections. Initially, these objections are typically framed as questions. And the most predictable question is this: "Why is there evil in the world? How can a just God permit pain and suffering?"

Notice that these questions are shorthand for larger arguments, but they are not themselves arguments. They are simply questions. The first step in response to this challenge is to *answer the question with a question*. Ask for a clearer definition of the problem and a statement of the precise argument they have in mind. This may not seem at first like a very promising way to begin, for it may suggest that you are completely oblivious to the possible theological ramifications of the reality of evil. But if we are to propose a solution to this great problem, we must be clear about the actual nature of the problem as it occurs in the mind of our objector. A vague, amorphous reference to something that could weigh against the existence of God will neither do justice to the gravity of the subject nor permit an adequate response. It is wise, therefore, not to accept the mere insinuation of an argument from evil. An objector should be prepared to spell out his objection with at least as much precision as he requires of your response.

Defining the Problem of Evil

You may wish to follow through a series of questions: "Is it that you think that God exists but that this God is neither trustworthy nor worthy of our affection? Or is it that you view belief in God as irrational? If so, why? How does the reality of suffering imply the nonexistence of God or the irrationality of belief in God?"

It is a good exercise for both parties to invite the objector to spell out the argument he envisions. And the believer needs to anticipate the possible responses to that invitation. One objector may say, "I can't really offer a straightforward argument." Another may fumble and piece together the lineaments of an argument, while voicing a sense of inadequacy: "I'm not doing this very well, but it goes something like this." Yet another type of response may come from the highly-prepared person who immediately produces premises and conclusions, with everything nicely laid out, neatly revealing the precise logic of the argument.

Suppose an objector struggles unsuccessfully to articulate an argument. With all diplomacy, you might then suggest that what is supposed to be obvious (namely, that evil implies the irrationality of belief in God) is not so obvious after all. Then you might offer your own clear formulation of the objection and ask, "Is that what you have in mind? Is that what is bothering you?" In other words, the best course of action may be to help the objector formulate the argument more precisely.

What does your willingness to help your partner in dialogue really communicate? It reflects integrity—not to mention credibility, preparation, and graciousness. And it opens doors. We break down barriers when we confess from our own human experience, "You know, I've thought a lot about this issue too. And I have to be honest with you, I've been bothered by this myself. So I can certainly understand your objection."

The beauty of this approach is summarized in the title of an older book on popular apologetics that I read as a college student: *I'm Glad You Asked.*[4] I've always loved that title; it's so at odds with our normal inclinations. How often do we secretly hope our non-Christian peers will *not* ask the questions they have because, after all, we are still processing the questions and answers for ourselves? With adequate preparation, though, we can be "glad when they ask," especially if the questions they raise ultimately provide a platform for presenting the gospel. One welcome aspect of the problem of evil is that it does invite an intelligent articulation of God's solution to the human predicament. We can speak of the hope of eternal life in Jesus and the divine solution to the problem of pain and suffering. Our attitude often betrays our doubts: "Why proclaim the gospel? Why bother? Nobody's listening. Nobody cares. Nobody wants to know." However, questions such as "Why is there evil in the world?" "How could God be real?" and "If God exists, what's He doing about pain and suffering?" throw open the door for us to share what we prematurely assume our listeners do not want to hear. So relish the questions for the opportunities they present.

Suppose your objector is able to lay out a compelling form of the argument from evil. What then? You must know what counts as a plausible form of the argument. For this purpose, it is helpful to turn to the literature in the philosophy of religion. There we have a record of the formulations of the argument that are taken seriously by those who have thought most deeply and persistently about the problem of evil.

Most philosophers of religion—atheists, agnostics, and theists alike—divide the major versions of the argument from evil against the existence of God into two categories: the *logical* and the *evidential* arguments. The relationship between these two terms needs some explanation, for the evidential argument is not *il*logical (as though "logic" and "evidence" were opposing terms). Rather, the terms simply refer to the manner in which each argument is constructed. Both methods are represented as plausible and compelling by their respective proponents.

The Logical Argument from Evil

What is "logical" about the logical argument from evil? "Logical" here refers to the deductive structure of this argument form. The argument is alleged to be formally valid, such that if the premises are true, the conclusion follows with such logical force that it also must be true. By the rules of logic, this is an argument of the strongest possible form. Syllogisms are common versions of deductive arguments. One type of syllogism is called *modus ponens*, which has the form:

If A, then B.
A.
Therefore, B.

Or, we could substitute for A and B to give a concrete example of this form:

Premise 1: If Socrates is a human being, then Socrates is mortal.
Premise 2: Socrates is a human being.
Conclusion: Therefore, Socrates is mortal.

Here's a syllogism of a slightly different form called *modus tollens*:

If A, then B.

Not B.
Therefore, not A.

With the same substitutions as before, we get the following argument:

Premise 1: If Socrates is a human being, then Socrates is mortal.
Premise 2: Socrates is not mortal.
Conclusion: Therefore, Socrates is not a human being.

Deductive arguments like these are logically impressive. If their respective premises are true, then their respective conclusions are necessarily true (i.e., they *cannot* be false). The formal strength of such arguments makes them quite daunting logically. If one accepts the premises of an argument where the conclusion follows validly from the premises, then the jig is up. One must accept the conclusion.

The ambition of the logical argument from evil is to demonstrate that God does not exist. However, as we'll see, the logical argument is so ambitious that this proves to be its Achilles' heel.

What does the logical argument from evil actually look like? Let me illustrate with a story, an experience I had when I was a college student. I was enrolled with about 100 other students in an elementary course in physics that we affectionately called "bonehead physics" (because not much brain power was required to succeed in the course). I thought of the professor as a cordial, gregarious sort of person, fairly popular with the students, even though I had never had a personal conversation with him. After class he would stand in the doorway and greet the students as they filed by, sort of like a Baptist minister following the Sunday sermon.

As I left class one day I overheard this professor talking with another student about religion. This piqued my curiosity. After listening from across the hall, I could tell that this professor of physics was genuinely and enthusiastically interested in religious questions. Standing there I thought, "I'm going to have to ask him about this." When the conversation concluded, I introduced myself and said, "You know, I overheard your conversation about religion. May I ask what is the nature of your interest in these questions?"

He answered, "I'm very sincere in seeking religious truth. I've been looking for religious reality and studying the major world religions for quite some time. It's been a major personal project for me, and I take the question of religious truth very seriously. But at this point I'm agnostic. I haven't reached any conclusions, and my quest continues." And then he corrected himself. "Actually," he said, "I have made some progress; I've narrowed the field slightly by eliminating one of the options. One major religious perspective I've considered just isn't reasonable. It's not plausible at all."

When he announced that it was Christianity that had failed the test of rational scrutiny, I thought it might be best just to drop the subject. But somehow the words just came out. "Really?" I said, "I'm a Christian, and I think I have some pretty good reasons for my beliefs. Would you be willing to tell me how you've concluded that Christianity can't be true?"

His answer was predictable and compact. "It all comes down to the problem of evil. First, Christians believe that God is all-powerful, or omnipotent. Second, they believe that God is morally perfect. Putting these together, if God is omnipotent he would desire to prevent evil if he wanted to, and if he is morally perfect he would desire to prevent evil if he could. Since the Christian God has both the desire to prevent evil and the power to fulfill that desire, there shouldn't be any evil at all. But obviously there is evil in the world. So the Christian God doesn't exist. It's that simple. That's why I'm not a Christian."

His statement of the problem was a version of the logical argument from evil. As he stated it, it is a *modus tollens* argument:

> Premise 1: If God (a Being that is both omnipotent and perfectly good) exists, then there should be no evil.
> Premise 2: But there is evil (i.e., it is not the case that there is no evil).
> Conclusion: God does not exist.

In effect, my professor of physics was arguing in a way made famous by Oxford philosopher J. L. Mackie.[5] He asserted that there is a *logical inconsistency* within the following set of three propositions accepted by most Christians: (1) God is omnipotent, (2) God is perfectly good, and (3) evil exists. The implications are severe. If these three propositions are logically incompatible, then the believer who seeks to be rational must abandon at least one of them in order to recover consistency in his beliefs. However, the Christian believer cannot abandon any one of these three propositions without ceasing to be fully Christian in what he believes. To deny evil, for example, would make mincemeat of the doctrine of the atonement of Jesus Christ in his death and resurrection. Without God's simultaneous love and power, the death of Jesus would be a meaningless symbol. And what, after all, would the crucified one be atoning for if not the evil that is so real and pervasive in human experience? The other propositions about divine omnipotence and moral perfection refer to major components in the Christian understanding of God's nature. They cannot be jettisoned either. Thus, proponents of the logical argument attempt to corner the believer into a logical "no-good-options" zone.

You may wonder what I said in response to my teacher. It was a moment of decision for me, and sometimes I think my philosophical career was launched during that conversation. With sincere respect for the superior fire-power of my professor, I acknowledged that I probably could not answer his objection to his satisfaction. Of course, he agreed. But he did say he would be interested in what I thought. For two hours we talked. My growing confidence peaked when this professor remarked at the end, "To be honest, some of this I really haven't thought through very well. You've raised some interesting questions, and you've given me some food for thought. Would you be willing to meet with me and a group of my university colleagues? I think they, too, would be interested in what you have to say." In total disbelief, the words fell from my trembling lips: "Okay, sure."

"Okay, sure." I was never more anxious in my life than during my preparations for the day of the planned gathering. But again God was gracious. My professor friend, after introducing me at the outset of the meeting, announced that we should all first agree about *what evil is* exactly. From that point the entire conversation focused on disagreement about the nature of evil. I never even had the opportunity to share what I had prepared to say! As I listened to sophisticated unbelievers first propose and then dispose of conflicting conceptions of evil operative in any plausible argument from evil against theism, it occurred to me that would-be objectors have their work cut out for them.

As for me, I resolved to wrestle further with this perennial objection in pursuit of the most compelling response. I've had twenty years to think about what I would say if I could sit down again with those gentlemen.[6]

How should we respond to the logical argument from evil, which charges Christian belief with logical inconsistency? There are several steps for dealing with the charge that a given set of propositions is inconsistent. On the face of it, these three propositions—asserting God's omnipotence, God's moral perfection, and the reality of evil—appear to be incompatible. The key question here is: "Is there any way to dispel the impression of inconsistency?"

A first step in dispelling the impression of inconsistency is to invite the objector to *demonstrate* the inconsistency of these propositions. Most thoughtful philosophers of religion acknowledge that the three propositions in question are not explicitly contradictory. They concede that, in order for the argument to be fully successful, it must be augmented with auxiliary premises. Additional propositions, acceptable to the Christian theist, are needed to draw out the alleged inconsistency. The needed supplements must specify what it means for God to be omnipotent and what it means for God to be morally perfect.

It turns out that producing the needed amplification is a daunting task in its own right. In fact, as most philosophers now agree, no objector has yet succeeded. We'll see why in a moment. But the point to grasp here is that the saber of the logical argument must have its edges sharpened with auxiliary propositions if it is to cut to the quick of theistic belief. Otherwise, the argument goes limp.

A second step, when confronted with the charge that a given set of propositions is logically inconsistent, is to offer reasons in support of the credibility of each individual proposition. If there is good reason to accept each proposition, then this is *prima facie* justification for affirming their conjunction. If our three propositions—God is omnipotent, God is morally perfect, and evil exists—are all independently plausible for good reasons, then the good reasons for believing each proposition *in isolation* are also good reasons to believe them *in conjunction*. And reasons to believe them in conjunction are reasons also to suppose that the appearance of contradiction is no more than *appearance*.

This consideration greatly reduces the impression of inconsistency. If an objector is made to *struggle* to support the charge of inconsistency, the point is even more powerful. For into the vacuum created by the difficulty of rigorously demonstrating a logical inconsistency one may insert evidence and credible reasons for taking each of the three propositions. This strategy also strengthens the believer's resolve to preserve commitment to orthodox belief rather than to adopt the compromising expedient of softening his position regarding the nature of God. Armed with evidence for the existence of God, the believer has a powerful means of parrying the thrust of this objection.[7]

A third step in dispelling the impression of inconsistency is most decisive. Here the goal is to demonstrate that the original set of three propositions is actually consistent.[8] Earlier I suggested that the Achilles' heel of the logical argument from evil is that it attempts the maximally ambitious project of demonstrating the nonexistence of God. But to demonstrate the nonexistence of God in this way, one must specify what is meant by divine omnipotence and divine moral perfection, and show that the conjunction of these properties entails the nonexistence of evil.

Let us consider each property in turn. The objector interprets divine omnipotence to mean that *God could prevent evil if He wanted to.* But is this a satisfactory characterization of divine omnipotence? Is it possible that there are worlds that God cannot create under certain conditions? Suppose God desires to create a world with free creatures who are capable of morally significant action. It is at least logically possible that even an omnipotent God may not be able to create such a world without also permitting evil. For in creating a world of creatures with freedom to do either good or evil, God leaves it up to them whether or not they will choose evil. Of course, because God is omniscient, He will know in advance whether a world with free creatures, able to do evil, would in fact be a world with evil in it. If God desires not to have a world with evil in it, He might choose not to create a world with free creatures. But having a world with free creatures may be a great enough good to justify God's creation of such a world, even if it is a world that He knows will contain evils caused by free creatures. The point is, if it is God's purpose to create a world with free creatures, His omnipotence does not entail that He can prevent free creatures from doing evil without violating their freedom. This broadening of the field of discussion through the exploration of logical possibilities challenges the assumption that an omnipotent God could prevent evil if he wanted to.

Next let us consider God's absolute moral perfection. The objector commonly interprets this to mean that *God would want to prevent evil if He could*. In response the theist may propose the following clarification of the doctrine of omnibenevolence: It is logically possible that a morally perfect God has *a morally sufficient reason for permitting all of the evils that exist*. The objector does not know that it is *not possible* that God has a morally justifiable reason for allowing every instance of suffering. What the absolute moral perfection of God actually implies is not that God must absolutely prevent evil, but that if God permits evil, then there must be some moral justification for His permission of it.

Notice, the theist is not required to *know* the specific "morally sufficient reasons" that would justify God's permission of evil. For the purposes of defusing the logical argument from evil, it is enough that the availability of morally sufficient reasons is a *logical possibility*. We need only propose that an all-powerful, all-loving God may in fact be morally justified in permitting every evil in the quantity that we actually find in the universe. The logical argument purports that divine moral perfection is logically incompatible with divine omnipotence and the reality of evil on the grounds that moral perfection entails the desire to prevent evil. But moral perfection only entails the prevention of evil that is not morally justified by some competing desire.

Here's an alternative way to make the same point. Suppose God is morally perfect. Suppose further that this entails that God (who is also omnipotent) would not permit any evil without having a morally sufficient reason for doing so. Then it follows that any actual evil is such that God is morally justified in permitting its occurrence. Again, this is true even if we cannot imagine what goods would justify God's permission of evils that occur. (Of course, we infer on the same grounds that God will see to it that worse evils—evils that would not be justified at all— never have and never will occur.)

Recall that the logical argument from evil is an *all-or-nothing* affair: either it is completely successful or it is an utter failure. Given the more plausible conceptions of divine omnipotence and divine moral perfection proposed in response to this objection, and the logical possibilities that these conceptions indicate, it follows that the logical argument does not demonstrate inconsistency among the three propositions in question. Thus, the argument fails completely. For the past three decades, proponents of the logical argument have been an endangered species.

The objector who still maintains that evil somehow counts against the rationality of Christian belief must abandon the logical argument in favor of a more promising line of attack.

The Evidential Argument from Evil

The above rebuttal of the logical argument from evil does not settle the question of rational belief in God. The skeptic may yet complain: "If God has morally sufficient reasons for permitting all the evils there are, we certainly do not know what those reasons are. In fact, it looks as if there are certain evils that simply are not morally justified."

This brings us to the evidential argument from evil. The chief premise of this argument is that *some evils are so bad that they (probably) are not morally justified.*[9]

Consider the multiple faces of evil and suffering. Some varieties may be regarded as just retribution for wrong actions; some persons are made to suffer because they deserve to be punished for wrong deeds. Other varieties of suffering may produce a good that could not be achieved by any other means, fostering in the sufferer greater faith in God, courage, and compassion towards others, and so forth. In these instances, we see how the evil permitted may be justified.

However, no matter how many different principles are set forth to explain the evils of our world, there will still remain a residue of evil, comprised of what we might consider the truly horrendous evils in the universe, that no one can explain. If there is some morally sufficient reason for God's permission of the greatest atrocities of human experience, it remains firmly hidden in the mind of God. We cannot conceive of goods that would justify such horrendous evils as those catalogued by Marilyn Adams: "individual and massive collective suffering . . . . the rape of a woman and axing off of her arms, psycho-physical torture whose ultimate goal is the disintegration of personality, betrayal of one's deepest loyalties, child abuse of the sort described by Ivan Karamozov, child pornography, parental incest, slow death by starvation, the explosion of nuclear bombs over populated areas."[10] (To this list I would add the orphaning of children through divorce.) Worse, it is unthinkable that any good could justify such evils; it is repugnant to us even to suppose that God's permission of the worst evils is somehow morally justified. Thus, even if it is logically possible that every instance of evil is permitted on morally sufficient grounds, our inability to make sense of certain evils is evidence that no such morally justifying reasons really exist. Even if we are mistaken in thinking that no morally sufficient reason justifies God's permission of truly horrendous evils, we are nevertheless rationally obliged to believe there is none *on the basis of the evidence we have.* Our evidence indicates that a morally sufficient reason does not exist. Since it is unlikely, as far as we can tell, that God has a morally justifying reason for permitting the worst kinds of evil, it is unlikely that an omnipotent and morally perfect being exists.

How are we to respond to this evidential argument from evil?

First, we may start by accounting for some classes of evil. Most people will grant that certain explanatory principles do adequately account for some of the evils in the world. There are certain goods that would not exist if evil were not permitted, even if the good of permitting certain other particular evils is unimaginable. How is this point helpful if the evidential argument appeals exclusively to the inexplicable evils of human experience? If, over time and in response to criticism, we develop a track record of offering plausible explanations for particular evils, then the residue of horrendous evils may be regarded as anomalies that have their own explanation even if we do not know what that explanation is. While this is not the strongest kind of response to the evidential argument, it is a helpful beginning.

Second, it is hardly surprising that there should be considerable mystery about the purposes of God. God Himself declares, "My thoughts are not your thoughts" (Isaiah 55:8). God's nature and ways are beyond our complete comprehension. It would be most unreasonable too expect to achieve perfect clarity about His purposes, His character, and His relationship to the world using the comparatively puny capacity for reflection that we have as finite creatures. If, after our most sophisticated deliberations, there remains some mystery that shrouds God's reasons for permitting some of the evils in the universe, does the lack of human comprehension really constitute a reason for believing that God has no morally sufficient reason for permitting those evils? The question answers itself.

Third, we must distinguish between *gratuitous evil* and *inscrutable evil*. Inscrutable evil is evil whose moral justification is beyond our (present) understanding. Gratuitous evil is evil that, as a matter of fact, occurs in the absence of any morally justifying reason. The major premise in the evidential argument is that there is gratuitous evil in the world. But what is the evidence for this? The only evidence for the existence of gratuitous evil is the evidence of inscrutable evil. But the existence of inscrutable evil certainly does not entail the existence of gratuitous evil. But perhaps inscrutable evil is good evidence for the existence of gratuitous evil. Let us consider this suggestion.

We have already noted the finitude of human understanding in judging God's purposes and actions. We have a limited capacity for discerning between *genuinely* gratuitous evil and only *apparently* gratuitous evil. Most skeptics know better than to claim that the existence of actually gratuitous evil can be demonstrated. The evidential argument from evil is thus *built upon the appearance of gratuitous evil*. But is that not at least a guide to rational belief on the part of cognitively limited human beings? Are we not dependent on how things appear or seem when we seek to make rational choices about what to believe? If we are not able, by our best efforts, to conceive of a plausible explanation for God's permission of horrendous evils, what can we do but conclude that there is no adequate explanation?

Certainly, appearances sometimes are adequate grounds for things we believe. This is generally the case in sensory perception, where how things appear in our visual field, for example, is a good indication of how things actually are. If I peer through the window and it seems visually to me that there is a white-headed pigeon on the telephone wire, then I probably am justified in believing that there is a pigeon on the wire. I am not justified in believing that there is a rhino on the wire. There are at least two reasons for this. First, I am not being appeared to in this way. It does not seem to me that there is a rhino on the wire. Second, even if I were appeared to in this way, I would have independent reason for thinking that there is something wrong with this appearance such that it is not a reliable indicator of the truth. For starters, rhinos are unknown to this part of southern California. Furthermore, rhinos

PHILOSOPHY: CHRISTIAN PERSPECTIVES FOR THE NEW MILLENNIUM

generally do not take much interest in scaling telephone poles (so, at least, I suspect). Nor do they have the capability of climbing telephone poles (of this I am certain).

But visual appearances are not always reliable grounds for belief. What if I report that it seems visually to me, from a distance of thirty meters, that there is an inchworm on the telephone wire? You would be right to doubt that I have the requisite powers of observation and that I jest when I offer such a report. It is doubtful that I should ever be appeared to in just that way. There may well be an inchworm on the wire. But if there is, it is highly unlikely that it would appear to me that there is. That is not the sort of thing I would be able to detect with the naked eye from a distance of thirty meters. In fact, as far as appearances are concerned, it (visually) appears to me that there is not an inchworm there.

Am I, then, justified in believing (as I now do, actually) that there is not an inchworm on the wire? Well, I am justified in believing this, but not on the basis of appearances. The belief policy I adopt with respect to the proposition that there is an inchworm on the telephone wire is grounded in other factors. In this case, the fact that I spontaneously and arbitrarily imagined the existence of an inchworm on the wire for the purposes of illustration is a major factor supporting my belief that the proposition is false. It would be a striking coincidence, would it not, if there actually was an inchworm right there, on precisely that spot on the wire, as I peer through the window while deliberately imagining just that circumstance? There may be other factors supporting my belief. But again, appearances have nothing to do with my judgment about the matter. The non-appearance of an inchworm is not evidence in support of my judgment that there is no inchworm there. You would be incredulous if I reported seeing an inchworm there; you should be equally incredulous if I report, "I believe there is no inchworm there because it visually appears to me that there is no inchworm there." On the other hand, if I say, "I believe there is not a pigeon on the wire because it visually appears to me that there is no bird of any sort on the wire," you may think me reasonable.

Now let us take the appearance of gratuitous evil. Is this more like the appearance that there is not a pigeon on the wire, or more like the appearance that there is not an inchworm on the wire? The skeptic assumes that the appearance of gratuitous evil is more like the appearance that there is no pigeon on the wire. But what is his basis for assuming that? The mere inscrutability of evil is not enough to warrant this assumption. The skeptic must have some conception of the powers of human understanding and the faculties appropriate to the discernment of gratuitous evils that permits his judgment that the appearance of evil is a reliable indicator of the actual existence of gratuitous evil. He would also have to know enough about the limits of moral justification for permitting evils to be sure that appearances of the absence of justifying reasons are an adequate indicator that there are no justifying reasons. He will be justified in believing there are no morally sufficient reasons for God's permission of apparently gratuitous evils only if appearances in this case are a reliable indication of the way things are. It begins to look like the skeptic must have God-like powers of cognition.

I believe it is question-begging even to assert, without more evidence than the mere inscrutability of evil, that there are *apparently* gratuitous evils in the world. We must be careful not to confuse the inability to discern a justifying reason with it seeming that there is no justifying reason. It is perfectly coherent for a theist to claim that it does not seem to him that any evil, no matter how inscrutable it may be, is gratuitous. It may, in fact, seem to the theist that no evil is gratuitous, even though some evils are admittedly inscrutable. His judgment that inscrutable evils do not appear to him to be gratuitous may rest on the confidence he has that God exists, that God is all-powerful and perfectly good, and that "in all things God works for the good" (Rom. 8:28). An unbeliever, lacking this conviction, is at most entitled to a cautious agnosticism about whether inscrutable evils are gratuitous. But this sort of agnosticism will not permit the confident denial that the existence of the worst evils makes the existence of God unlikely and belief in God irrational. The force of the evidential argument evaporates.

Some Final Considerations

We have explored the two most prominent forms of the argument from evil against God's existence. As it happens, there is a little-appreciated argument from evil *for* the existence of God. It begins with the question that stumped my physics professor and his cohorts:

"What is evil?" I think the most intuitively plausible, non-question-begging answer is that evil is *a departure from the way things ought to be*. We call certain events "evil" because they seem to be a breakdown in the way things ought to be. When we hear of the brutal, senseless, and intentional slaying of an innocent person, we naturally recoil in horror and insist, "That's just not right!" We do not feel that we are merely expressing an opinion or a preference. We are making a judgment about objective reality. But if evil is a departure from the way things ought to be, then it follows that there is a way things ought to be in order for there to be evil. But here's the rub for the unbeliever: How can there be a way things *ought* to be unless there is a *design plan* for the world? And how can there be a design plan without a suitably talented, intelligent, powerful, resourceful designer and fashioner of contingent reality? We humans can be very smug about the theological implications of evil because it makes us wonder if God really cares. But what does it mean to insist that God does not exist, if our conviction that evil exists is so irresistible? Atheists and agnostics have their own problem of evil to contend with.

Furthermore, those who repudiate religious belief because of evil trivialize suffering and the admirable and enviable faith of those who suffer, especially when those who suffer remain faithful and find reason for hope in the face of suffering on account of God's presence and goodness to them. It is rather more puzzling when a person of naturalistic orientation suffers with grace and courage. To what do they attribute their endurance in suffering? What is the source of their strength? Is it not easier to make sense of the source of courage, comfort, and grace for a believer in God who suffers? The skeptic who ridicules the conviction that God exists and that God has morally sufficient reasons for permitting horrendous evils tacitly mocks the vibrant, authentic faith of true believers who experience horrendous evils and yet come to love and trust God even more. Perhaps the depth of conviction among believers who suffer is a signpost pointing to a reality that the unbeliever has yet to experience.

The crowning consideration in our response to the problem of evil is that God has done something about evil. He himself passes through it, experiences it, and defeats it. In Peter Kreeft's book on popular Christian apologetics, *Yes or No: Straight Answers to Tough Questions About Christianity*, a Christian and an unbeliever are engaged in dialogue about the truth of Christianity. Addressing the problem of evil, the Christian remarks:

> He [Jesus Christ] came right down into our trap and died to free us. The One who asks us to trust Him to solve the problem of evil already did the greatest thing to conquer it. He suffered every kind of evil with us. He was hated by the people He loved. He was nailed to a cross and died. He even felt His father leave him horribly alone on the cross when he said, "My God, my God, why have You forsaken Me?" *That's* evil. All the evil in the world is there, and there He is in the middle of it. You think of God up in Heaven controlling things down here and you wonder why He doesn't do a better job. You wonder if He really cares, and how He can be good if He just stays there and turns away and lets terrible things happen. But it's not like that. He didn't stay away. He came down into evil. That's the Christian answer to the problem of evil. Not a tricky argument, but Christ on the cross, God on our side, the side of the innocent sufferer.[11]

And then he says these most memorable words: "How can you resent a God like *that?*"

Some time ago I debated the question, "Does God exist?" with an agnostic philosopher and friend of mine. During the question-and-answer session afterward, one woman approached the microphone and with obvious rage began to explain why her experience with pain and suffering prevented her from believing that God exists. It was as if she blamed me for this because I believed in God.

As tactfully as I could, I said to her, "I can't help but notice that you seem very angry. But with whom are you angry, if God does not exist? Are you angry with me for believing in God? How does that help you? The real question is: 'Are you sure you don't believe in God?' Perhaps it isn't that you don't believe in God, but that you're angry with God. But consider what God has done for you through Jesus Christ. Can you really resent a God like that?"

When we reach this level of dialogue with co-sufferers in the human community, we begin to touch the deepest existential problem of all and connect our own universal human experience of suffering and evil with God's redemptive purposes.[12]

---

[1] Victor Hugo, *Les Misérables*, trans. Lee Fahnestock and Norman MacAfee (New York: Signet/Penguin Books, 1987), 94-95.

[2] All biblical citations are from *The New International Version.*

[3] Thomas Watson, *All Things for Good* (1663; Edinburgh/Carlisle, Pa: Banner of Truth, 1986, repr.), 27.

[4] Ken Boa and Larry Moody, *I'm Glad You Asked* (Wheaton, Ill.: Victor Books, 1987, repr.).

[5] See J. L. Mackie, "Evil and Omnipotence," Mind 64 (1955): 200-12; and ch. 9 in his *The Miracle of Theism* (Oxford: Clarendon Press, 1982).

[6] My first published book grew out of this experience. See *Evil and the Evidence for God* (Philadelphia: Temple University Press, 1993).

[7] For a detailed argument on this point, see my *Evil and the Evidence for God.*

[8] Portions of the discussion that follows parallel Alvin Plantinga's treatment of this argument in his book *The Nature of Necessity* (Oxford: Clarendon Press, 1974), ch. 9.

[9] For a seminal exposition of the evidential argument, see William L. Rowe, "The Problem of Evil and Some Varieties of Atheism," in *Contemporary Perspectives on Religious Epistemology*, ed. R. Douglas Geivett and Brendan Sweetman (New York: Oxford University Press, 1992). For a sampling of sophisticated reflection on the evidential argument by prominent figures in philosophy of religion, see *The Evidential Argument from Evil*, ed. Daniel Howard-Snyder (Bloomington, Ind.: Indiana University Press, 1996). An excellent and accessible treatment of the evidential argument is James Petrik's *Evil Beyond Belief* (Armonk, N.Y./London: M. E. Sharpe, 2000).

[10] Marilyn McCord Adams, *Horrendous Evils and the Goodness of God* (Ithaca, NY: Cornell University Press, 1999), 26.

[11] Peter Kreeft, *Yes or No? Straight Answers to Tough Questions about Christianity* (Ann Arbor, MI: Servant Books, 1984), 41.

[12] I wish to thank my assistant, John Kwak, for his help in preparing the manuscript for this chapter.

Chapter Eight

———≈≈≈≈———

HUMAN NATURE AND THE SEARCH FOR GOD

Paul Copan

Dr. Paul Copan is a frequent lecturer on university campuses with Ravi Zacharias International Ministries (Norcross, Georgia) and is Visiting Associate Professor at Trinity International University (Deerfield, Illinois). He is author of "True for You, But Not for Me" (Bethany House) and "That's Just Your Interpretation" (Baker).

Abstract

"God isn't content with our simply acknowledging his existence or having justified true belief that he exists. God wants us to embrace him as our loving Father and Lord. God wants us to know and love him—not just know he exists. We can't separate those two questions. . . . Our personal response must complement the evidence. At the heart of our very existence is the important consideration of responding to a God who has loving and sufficiently revealed himself and who will allow us to know him if we humble ourselves before him."

I N THE MOVIE LOVE AND DEATH, BORIS Dimitrovich (Woody Allen) discusses what nature is all about with Sonya (Diane Keaton), the girl he loves. Looking at a large symmetrical leaf, Sonya asks in wonderment, "Isn't it incredible?"

Boris replies, "To me nature is—I don't know—spiders and bugs, big fish eating little fish . . . animals eating animals. It's like one enormous restaurant. That's the way I see it."

Sonya continues, "But if there is no God, then life has no meaning. Why go on living? Why not just commit suicide?" To this Boris replies: "Well, let's not get hysterical; I could be wrong. I'd hate to blow my brains out and then read in the papers they'd found something."

Is Boris right? Are we just left to survive in this cosmic "restaurant" into which we've been accidentally placed? As Boris asked later on, "What if we're a bunch of absurd people running around with no rhyme or reason?"

Introduction: The Problem of Meaning

When we talk about *meaning*, we are implying some *purpose*. *Meaning is dependent upon or derivative from some purpose.* If I happen to be looking at the sky, and I make out the formation of the letters G-O-L-D in a consecutive cluster of clouds, I have no good reason to think that this is anything but coincidental. I have no reason to think to think there is a connection between the clouds and the existence of gold (say, buried in my backyard). There is no *meaning* in this formation since there was no purpose or intention to serve as the appropriate context for it.[1]

We believe that even though language refers to certain truths and realities, it is still conventional. That is, people have *agreed* upon certain symbols meaning certain things. So the word *gift* in English has a positive connotation, but *Gift* in German (poison) has a negative one. The *purpose* of the community of speakers has given *meaning* to words. The word *gift* in and of itself does not have *intrinsic meaning*.

151

The question that we at some point have to ask ourselves is this: Is there any true and objective meaning to our lives? Is there a meaning to *discover*, or do we simply *invent* it? Are we a bunch of absurd people running around with no rhyme or reason?

There are some people who say, "Even though the universe—and more specifically, the human race—*as a whole* does not have meaning, *my own life* can still have meaning." But it seems to me that if there is no ultimate meaning to life in general, why should I think that *my* life could be full of meaning in any non-arbitrary sense? For example, why should I think that what Mother Teresa did is truly meaningful whereas prostitution, child abuse or serial-killing is not—even if it gives fulfillment to some people? The person who claims that life can be objectively meaningful without there being some ultimate purpose for human beings must show how this is so.

Now some atheistic thinkers have recognized, however, that consistency demands meaninglessness entirely. Bertrand Russell made the connection between the fact that "man is the product of causes that had no prevision of the end they were achieving. That his origin, his growth, his hopes and fears, his loves, his beliefs, are but the outcome of accidental collocations of atoms" *and* "the firm foundation of unyielding despair," upon which "the soul's habitation" can be "safely built."[2]

Now even if we take Russell's viewpoint, we still tend to live as though our lives have meaning—that we *ought* to care for our children, that there are certain ways of life (being a caring schoolteacher) that are better than others (being a drug addict). It seems as though *implicitly* we recognize life as somehow having meaning.

Someone may object: Simply because we *long* for meaning and purpose does not imply that meaning and purpose exist. Something does not *become* meaningful just because we *wish* it so or because we find the alternatives less than desirable.

But consider this: The fact that we long for meaning and purpose and coherence to our lives *may be an indication* that something transcendental and beyond ourselves actually does exist. For example, it is not uncommon to hear some people say: "You just believe in God because you are seeking security. You need some father-figure in your life to give you comfort in a cold and heartless world." The problem with this is that this doesn't in any way show whether God exists or not. It just shows how some people may have come to believe in God. Furthermore, one could respond, "And maybe you *reject* God because you are resisting having a father-figure in your life." The sword cuts both ways, and we must be careful of moving into the *psychology* of belief and away from the *rationality* of belief in God. The more important question is: *are there good reasons to believe in God?* rather than *what motivates you to believe (or disbelieve) in God?*

But there's another problem: Why should *need* imply that it is somehow wrong or illegitimate? We human beings need food and drink, but this does not mean that eating and drinking are somehow wrong? Rather, our bodies function properly when they have food. Could it not be that we as human beings function properly when our lives are rightly aligned with God and his purposes?

The French philosopher Blaise Pascal said that we human beings have been made with a God-shaped hole that only God can fill. Pascal pointed out the foolishness of trying to fill that hole with things like education, prestige, power, sex, money. But since the hole within us is God-shaped, these lesser things can never satisfy in any ultimate sense.

The Danish philosopher Søren Kierkegaard said that we humans are a mixed-bag—namely, we are creatures who are both temporal and "eternal" (or *transcendent-oriented*). We cannot fulfill our nature when we live as though this earthly life is all that there is. One can live a wasteful life of gluttony, drunkenness, and sexual license, but such a life is doomed to frustration. One lives from one sensual experience to the next, seeking to improve upon the past pleasure but never finding satisfaction. But even if we go to the next level of mere-earthly existence by enjoying fine intellectual and cultural pleasures—attending plays, reading heady books, enjoying rich literature, delighting ourselves with fine music, we shall still miss out on a primary feature of our intrinsic nature. If we live as though this earthly life is all that there is—whether as hedonistic or refined persons, such an existence cannot ultimately satisfy.

Why not? Perhaps we get a clue by the kinds of questions that have concerned human beings throughout the ages. We are creatures who seek *explanations* and *coherence* to life. We ask questions such as: Who am I? Where have I come from? Where am I going? What is my purpose—if I have one?

We resist contradiction because we know in our minds that self-contradictory systems cannot be true. We resist any fragmented explanations because incoherence is an assault on what makes us function properly as human beings. We tend to look for coherence. Huston Smith, the noted author on world religions, has said that when a worldview results in meaninglessness, isolation, and anxiety, this is an indication of a poor fit between our minds and reality. When there is a good fit, however, this will most likely be evidenced by the world's making sense.[3]

What I want to point out is that *theism* has greater explanatory power, a better fit, than alternative worldviews or outlooks on life and is therefore more likely to be true. What I mean by theism is that there exists a personal, good Creator and Sustainer of the universe, and we human beings are his creation. We have been made in God's image. That is, we have been made to resemble him in certain limited ways so that we may know God and may relate to one another in deep and meaningful ways. The image of God involves our possession of dignity and worth. Such worth is evidenced by the fact that we are personal, moral, rational, self-conscious, and volitional beings. So we cannot separate the question of God's existence from the matter of his purposes for us.

Let's look more closely at two of theism's major tenets: (1) a personal God exists and (2) God has made us in his image.

A Personal Creator Exists[4]

The old Taoist question—"How do I know whether I'm a man dreaming he's a butterfly or a butterfly dreaming it's a man?"—has been taken seriously by many. But, at the risk of appearing to be unnecessarily dismissive, let me say this: I am *justifiably* assuming that the physical universe exists and is not simply illusory (as some Eastern philosophies claim). From an intuitive and commonsense point of view, there seems to be no good reason to deny what seems so obvious to all of us. Even if we may *theoretically* accept the phenomenal world and the distinctions within it as illusory, our *practical* experiences of eating pizza, driving in traffic, and interacting with other embodied persons offers what I believe to be a strong counterpoint to this illusionist position.

The Beginning of the Universe Points Us
to a Personal Cause of the Universe

Why does the universe exist? How did it come into existence? Did it merely pop into existence by nothing and from nothing? Atheist philosopher of science Quentin Smith believes that the universe caused itself; other philosophers claim that the universe came into existence out of nothing.[5] Now according to implications of relativity theory, all the space, time, matter, and energy did not exist "prior" to the Big Bang. The universe was shrunk down to nothing at all. How can something come out of nothing—when there is not even any potential for the formation and existence of something? *From nothing, nothing comes.* The theist affirms the commonly accepted intuitive and obvious belief that whatever *begins* to exist has a cause.

When asked where the universe came from, Bertrand Russell simply said "the universe is just there, and that's all."[6] But why is there something rather than nothing at all? As physicist Paul Davies reminds us: "There is not a shred of evidence that the universe is logically necessary."[7] Yet the theist maintains that the reason there is something rather than nothing at all is due to a Creator who fits the Judeo-Christian understanding of a Being who brought the universe into existence.[8]

Furthermore, the universe is winding down, as physicist Stephen Hawking claims, such that it is approaching the "Big Crunch."[9] It has been wound up, and it is winding down until the universe suffers a heat death.[10] Everything within the universe is contingent—it has not always been here. There is no reason to think the universe necessarily exists. There must be something on which the universe depends.[11] If everything within the universe is dependent, then we are pointed towards something on which the universe depends.

If there was once no space-time world, what brought something from nothing? A personal being who freely chose to bring about the finite world offers a very plausible and likely explanation. Now some may say that this is not a scientific explanation. But why should this be a problem? We as personal agents act freely all the time—that is, we have a model for how personal agency works without appealing to science. Why then couldn't this serve as the basis for claiming that a divine personal Being could also creatively act?

The Fine-Tuning of the Universe Points Us to an Intelligent Cause

If the universe's delicately balanced conditions (e.g., rate of expansion; balance of nuclear, electromagnetic, or gravitational forces; etc.) were only slightly altered, life would be impossible. The universe is so finely-tuned that it is "just right" for human life ("the Goldilocks effect"). The likelihood of *life-prohibiting* universes is vastly greater than *life-permitting* ones, let alone a *life-producing* one. Many cosmic constants are so delicately balanced that if any one of them were to be slightly altered, no life would be possible.

What are some of these?

- For biological life to be possible, over 40 different elements must be able to bond together to form molecules. This bonding is based on the strength of electromagnetic force and the ratio of the mass of the electron to that of the proton.

- "[I]f the force of gravity were even slightly stronger, all stars would be blue giants [which burn too briefly for life to develop]; if even slightly weaker, all would be red dwarfs [these are too cold to support life-bearing planets]."[12] Under such conditions, there would be no life. If the force of gravity were slightly different, no habitable planets would exist.

- A .01% increase during the early stages of the Big Bang would have yielded a "present-day expansion thousands of times faster than what we find. An equivalent decrease would have led to recollapse when the cosmos was a millionth its present size."[13]

- If the gravitational pull of Big Bang were to increase as little as 2% in strength, hydrogen atoms could not exist, making life impossible. (All hydrogen would become helium.)[14]

Non-theistic astronomers John Barrow and Joseph Silk state that the universe is "unexpectedly hospitable to life."[15] It is "a surprisingly complex place"[16] and is "tailor-made for life."[17] They go so far as to admit that our new picture of the universe "is more akin to the traditional metaphysical picture of creation out of nothing."[18]

In the *Scientific American* Freeman Dyson notes: "As we look out into the Universe and identify the many accidents of physics and astronomy that have worked together for our benefit, it almost seems as if the Universe must in some sense have known that we were coming."[19] Thus, we're pointed in the direction of an intelligent mind and powerful agent.

Philosopher John Leslie, one of the foremost authorities on the universe's fine-tuning and not a believer in God, states that "the God hypothesis is a viable alternative"[20] to explain this delicate balance of the universe's conditions for life. A theistic explanation shouldn't be ruled out; in fact, it becomes more plausible given that naturalism can in no way predict such a finely-tuned universe, whereas given theism, we can expect such an outcome.[21]

It is ironic that many atheists speak of the "God of the gaps"—that science has gradually squeezed out God as because God is no longer needed to explain anything in the natural world. This is simply not true. In the past century, we have seen two significant areas of scientific discovery where a personal, intelligent, and powerful God offers a more plausible explanation than its naturalistic counterparts— the beginning of the universe and the fine-tuning of the universe for human life. These recent developments certainly didn't surprise believers in God.

Furthermore, present naturalistic attempts to account for this delicate balance are just as metaphysical as theism, and it seems that these theories are so entrenched in naturalism that no matter how intricate and apparently designed the universe is, many of these naturalistic scientists would never admit to divine design.

But the theist is certainly rational in believing in an Intelligent Designer—not simply an impersonal Force or Reality. We are pointed in the direction of the theistic *God*, a personal creator whose creation is distinct from him. Even if we don't have expansive knowledge about this Being (as all-knowing, all-powerful, all-good, etc.), we have *sufficient* awareness and evidence to be held accountable to him and—via reason and revelation—to investigate more fully the nature of this Being.

Humans as God's Image-Bearers

We Possess Dignity and Worth

The philosopher Immanuel Kant (d. 1804) spoke of the importance and necessity of treating persons as *ends*, rather than as *means* to an end. Despite our apparent insignificance in the vast universe, human beings possess an intrinsic dignity:

> Two things fill the mind with ever new and increasing admiration and awe, the oftener and more steadily we reflect on them: the starry heavens above me and the moral law within me. . . . The former view of a count-less multitude of worlds annihilates, as it were, my importance as an animal creature, which must give back to the planet (a mere speck in the universe) the matter from which it came, the matter which is for a little time provided with vital force, we know not how. The latter, on the contrary, infinitely raises my worth as that of an intelligence by my personality, in which the moral law reveals a life independent of all animali-ty and even of the whole world of sense—at least so far as it may be inferred from the purposive destination assigned to my existence by this law, a destination which is not restricted to the conditions and limits of this life but reaches into the infinite.[22]

Human beings have intrinsic value, not instrumental value; they are not mere objects to be used but are ends in themselves.

By contrast, Nobel Prize winner Francis Crick declares in his book *The Astonishing Hypothesis* that human beings are organisms physiologically determined to act as they do:

> The Astonishing Hypothesis is that 'You,' your joys
> and your sorrows, your memories, and your ambitions,
> your sense of personal identity and free will, are in fact
> no more than the behavior of a vast assembly of nerve
> cells and their associated molecules. . . . This hypothesis
> is so alien to the ideas of most people alive today that
> it can truly be called astonishing.[23]

If Crick is right, then his book is nothing more than a vast assembly of
nerve cells and their associated molecules! But isn't Crick acting like he's
more than this? And in the depths of our being, don't we believe that
we have value as persons, that our relationships are important, that we
are rightly offended and insulted when people treat us like dirt? No
matter what our philosophy of life (whether the naturalism of the West
or the monism of the East), we admit to human personhood and dignity
in our day-to-day living.

The Japanese poet Issa (1762-1826), one of the best loved Haiku
poets, endured a very sad life. All of his five children died before he was
thirty. After one of their deaths, he went to a Zen master and asked for
some advice to help him make sense out of suffering. The master told
him that the world is just like the dew, which evaporates when the sun
shines upon it. Life is transient, and to grieve such loss and desire something
more is a failure to transcend one's own selfish desires. Despite this
philosophical answer, Issa recognized that there is something more than
such an impersonal explanation. He wrote this poem:

> This Dewdrop World—
> A dewdrop world it is,
> And yet,
> And yet . . . .[24]

It seems that a view that diminishes individuality and personality
diminishes a very real aspect of human existence. Issa's philosophy
depersonalized his loss—that the world is dew. But his experience
seemed to contradict this—the loss of this father, this human being, was
real and personal. From the theistic point of view, our individuality and
personality and the personal attachments we are capable of forming are

not an inherent problem. These have been created by God as good, but the problem is when self is misdirected and pursues the wrong ends and sets its mind on what is evil. Theism affirms the goodness of human individuality and personality because God himself is personal. *Thus there is the basis for affirming the personal worth of individual human beings.*

We Are Moral Beings

Objective moral values exist, and we can intuitively recognize that certain acts are right or wrong such as murder, theft, torture, or rape. And when cultures engage in human sacrifice or treachery, then at this point their morality is defective or non-existent.

Even many atheists recognize this. Kai Nielsen claims that acts such as wife-beating and child molestation are "vile." He asserts:

> It is more reasonable to believe such elemental things to be evil than to believe any skeptical theory that tells us we cannot know or reasonably believe any of these things to be evil. . . . I firmly believe that this is bedrock and right and that anyone who does not believe it cannot have probed deeply enough into the grounds of his moral beliefs.[25]

The philosopher J. P. Moreland tells the story of an illuminating encounter with a relativistic student at the University of Vermont. J.P. was speaking in a dorm room, and a student who lived in that room said, "Whatever is true for you is true for you and whatever is true for me is true for me. If something works for you because you believe it, that's great. But no one should force his or her views on other people since everything is relative."[26] J.P. told him that his view implied that there was no such thing as sin or wrongdoing. As J.P. left, he unplugged the student's stereo and started out the door with it.

The student protested: "Hey, what are you doing? . . . . You can't do that!"

J.P. replied, "You're not going to *force* on me the belief that it is wrong to steal your stereo, are you?"

When it's convenient, people will say they don't care about sexual morality or cheating on exams, but they become moral absolutists in a hurry when someone steals their things. We really do believe in morality—no matter what we claim to believe philosophically.

Authors Randy Thornhill and Craig Palmer have argued in their book, *A Natural History of Rape*, that rape is "natural." It happens in nature (for example, male mallard ducks "rape"), and this rape can be explained biologically. That is, male genes make males rape. Why? Because of the innate drive to reproduce and survive, to pass on their genes. Thornhill and Palmer call rape "an adaptive reproductive strategy."

So when males fail to attract a mate, they rape as a last resort. There is an often-unconscious desire to impregnate. So rape, rather than being pathological or an act of violence, comes from the desire to procreate. So even if it's not nice, it's certainly *natural*.

There are objective moral facts (Nazi or Stalinist brutalities, widow burning, torture). We intuitively recognize such truths as "torturing babies for fun is wrong"; "murder or theft is wrong"; "kindness is good." There seems no good reason to reject these intuitions—any more than we would deny our sense of perception—even if we don't always see as accurately as we should (e.g., we see apparent wetness on the pavement, but it turns out to be a mirage). Furthermore, our moral understanding can be refined and honed—just as with our visual or auditory acuity (e.g., learning to track animals).

Some say that we can't make moral judgments because there are differing moral systems. Yet one could ask what is the *basis* of this knowledge statement. Also, if a person says that we *ought* not make moral judgments or that we *ought* to remain neutral about moral systems, then she has introduced a moral judgment into the discussion. Moreover, it doesn't logically follow that because there are different expressions of morality between cultures, objective moral values don't exist. The "plurality argument" (that differing moral systems prove that there is no universal objective ethic) won't work. What if you have different answers to a question on a math exam? Because there are differences, this doesn't mean the answers are all correct or legitimate.[27] Furthermore, *the hardening of conscience* is an important consideration when it comes to some divergences on the topic of morality.

But do we really doubt *right now* that it's wrong to murder or rape or commit adultery? If people think that such actions are relative, they haven't reflected very deeply on morality. Often, they are just being selective about what moral values they choose to hold to. Indeed, it is ironic that those who are moral relativists are also those who would likely speak of having "rights" or "freedom." But why respect rights if everything is relative? Why think one *ought* to have regard for another's freedom of speech or religion when one has the power to suppress it?

My wife and I were at a dinner in Washington, DC. We were chatting with a married couple. The husband told me he was a relativist—that there are ultimately no moral norms to follow. "Whatever is right for you is right for you, and whatever is right for me is right for me." I got the attention of his wife and said to her: "Your husband believes that it's okay if he commits adultery." She glared at him. I explained: "He told me that there is no right and wrong, which must mean that it's ultimately okay to cheat on you." She said, "I'd like to hear him explain." He had a sudden conversion experience and told us, "Well, there are certainly *some* things that are wrong."

Furthermore, those who get upset at "imposing" morality on others apparently believe that it is morally wrong to impose morality on others. But why get so uptight if everything is relative, if objective moral values don't exist? The fact that even relativists get upset and offended at "intolerance" or "bigotry" implies a moral standard that is being violated.

I was speaking on a university campus, where I was accused of being ethnocentric because of what I believed about morality—that certain things are right and certain things are wrong and that I was imposing my views on others. But isn't it *universally* wrong to be ethnocentric?

I then asked the student—who happened to be a young woman: "If you were about to be raped, and you saw a bystander, would you want the bystander to impose his morality on your attacker." I said, "It's easy to be a moral relativist when it comes to generalizations and *other* cultures. But when faced with evil personally, we have greater moral clarity."

To say that another culture's practices are *immoral* is not cultural arrogance if there is the recognition of moral flaws within one's own culture (as well as the virtues within other cultures). Furthermore, to assume that I cannot "make judgments" about another actually undermines the possibility of moral reform (e.g., abolishing slave trade, civil rights for minorities).

Just as those who deny the objectivity of basic logical laws (identity or non-contradiction) need special help, so do those who deny basic moral intuitions about the wrongness of murder or the rightness of kindness.

We Possess Self-Consciousness

Philosophers of science have recognized that it is exceedingly difficult to account for consciousness if the natural world is all there is. How could completely physical processes produce consciousness—whether in non-human animals or human beings?

The philosopher of mind Ned Block forcefully asserts:

> We have no conception of our physical or functional nature that allows us to understand how it could explain our subjective experience . . . [I]n the case of consciousness we have nothing—zilch—worthy of being called a research programme, nor are there any substantive proposals about how to go about starting one. . . . Researchers are *stumped.*"[28]

Similarly, the materialist philosopher of mind Colin McGinn writes:

> How is it possible for conscious states to depend upon brain states? How can technicolour phenomenology arise from soggy grey matter? . . .How could the aggregation of millions of individually insentient neurons generate subjective awareness? We know that brains are the *de facto* causal basis of consciousness, but we have, it seems, no understanding of how this can be so. It strikes us as miraculous, eerie, even faintly comic.[29]

The emergence of consciousness is deeply problematic for the naturalist, and to base the emergence of moral properties on an appeal to the emergence of consciousness from matter is grossly ill-conceived. Again, we cite McGinn:

> Consider the universe before conscious beings came along: the odds did not look good that such beings could come to exist. The world was all just physical objects and physical forces, devoid of life . . . . We have a good idea of how the Big Bang led to the creation of stars and galaxies, principally by force of gravity. But we know of no comparable force that might explain how ever-expanding lumps of matter might have developed into conscious life.[30]

So where do we go? Unlike non-human animals, human beings are not only conscious, but self-conscious. They are aware that they aware. But how do we best account for the existence of such awareness?

The theist suggests that human beings have been made by a supremely aware Being. A God who knows, who thinks, who sees with the eyes of his mind. A theistic explanation for this phenomenon is more "natural" than naturalism.

We Are Volitional Beings

We human beings like choices: thirty-one ice cream flavors at Baskin-Robbins; huge malls with incredible selections for consumption; huge home and garden warehouses such as Home Depot—the list goes on. We also act as though we can make free and responsible choices. When we look at a menu and select one dish over against other palatable ones, we believe that our choices make a difference, that we are self-determining agents, that we could have chosen differently.

God has made us with the power to choose, to make choices. We intuitively believe that we have freedom to choose between alternatives. Even those who claim that everything is determined don't really believe that their conclusion was determined. It's no wonder: we've been made in God's image.

During an open forum at Worcester Polytechnic Institute in Massachusetts, a student challenged me: "Try to disprove this thesis: All that we do is an attempt to survive." I replied, "Are you asking this question because you want to survive or is it because you want to know the truth of the matter? Because if you just want to survive, there are probably plenty of beliefs that will help us as a species to survive—believing that human beings have dignity and rights, that objective moral values exist and should be heeded. We may strongly believe these things because of socio-biological evolution, but they may be completely false." I then went on: "I'll bet that you want to do more than just survive. You've been made in the image of a good and loving—but rational—God. You've been made for more than just survival. You're a rational being. You've been made for seeking and finding truth—even if it doesn't contribute to your physical survival."

If God exists and wants us human beings to freely know him and love him, it seems that two things would likely be true: (a) There would be evidence available to all people and that they would not need Ph.D.s in order to infer God's existence. (b) This evidence could be rationalized away, that one could find loopholes if one wanted to. That is, good evidence is available, but not all may be looking for it because there is also a personal dimension to knowing God.

I'm married and have five children. I don't know how I would *prove beyond the shadow of a doubt* that I'm married—I could show you my wedding band, my marriage license, wedding pictures—and even introduce you to my wife, but all of this could be explained away by sharp minds. In other words, even though I've made a sufficient and reasonable case for my being married, you could still find loopholes.

Loyola University philosopher Paul Moser has told of an atheist friend who said he would *kill* himself if he had to acknowledge God's reality.[31] Despite evidence for God's existence, people may not *want* to look for that evidence. And then they throw up their hands and say, "I just don't have enough evidence for God's existence." But we must remember that there are two kinds of ignorance—one for which we can't be held responsible and another for which we can. I may be ignorant about the speed limit because I wasn't paying attention, but I can't tell the highway patrol that I'm not guilty. A precondition for driving on the road is attentiveness to its rules and protocols.

Many atheists and skeptics are uncritically dismissive of evidence for God's existence. They sometimes suggest: "If arguments fail to show, with deductive conclusiveness, that the maximally-great Creator of the universe exists, then I'm not interested." If the kinds of arguments offered above are minimally successful, however, then we still live in what Dallas Willard calls an "ontologically haunted universe."[32] This would reasonably call for further probing, even whole-hearted seeking, rather than casual dismissal. Much is at stake, including our own futures, in the perennial issue of God's reality.[33]

If God exists, then God cannot simply be the topic of armchair conversations. God does not exist for the purposes of our intellectual stimulation or entertainment. If God exists and is a self-revealing Being, and if we have been designed for a loving relationship with God, then a searching, thoughtful, and humble heart is fitting as we commence the examination. As Blaise Pascal writes: "My whole heart strains to know what the true good is in order to pursue it: no price would be too high to pay for eternity."[34]

There are good reasons to think that theism is true and that who we are reflects who God is—in our dignity, personality, morality, consciousness, and volition. Theism offers important answers to our deepest questions—both intellectually and experientially. How can *conscious, personal, moral, valuable beings* emerge from non-conscious, impersonal, non-moral, valueless processes? Naturalism has no answers where theism does. Theism gives coherent answers, but God will only take us so far since the response is up to us: "Choose this day whom you will serve."

God isn't content with our simply acknowledging his existence or having justified true belief that he exists. God wants us to embrace him as our loving Father and Lord. God wants us to know and love him—not just know he exists. We can't separate those two questions. Once we do personally respond to this God, we find strength to live life the way it was designed to be lived. To those willing to take him very seriously, God promises: "'*When you search for me, you will find me; if you seek me with all your heart, I will let you find me,*' says the Lord."[35] Our personal response must complement the evidence. At the heart of our very existence is the important consideration of responding to a God who has loving and sufficiently revealed himself and who will allow us to know him if we humble ourselves before him.

[1] See Thomas Morris, *Making Sense of It All* (Grand Rapids: Eerdmans, 1992), 47-62.

[2] Bertrand Russell, "A Free Man's Worship," in *Mysticism and Logic and Other Essays* (London: Allen & Unwin, 1963), 41.

[3] Huston Smith, "The Religious Significance of Postmodernism: A Rejoinder," *Faith and Philosophy* 12 (July 1995): 415.

[4] The fact of consciousness/subjectivity, intentionality, and various mental properties: New York University philosopher and atheist Thomas Nagel writes, "Consciousness is what makes the mind-body problem really intractable." "What Is It Like To Be a Bat?" *Philosophical Review* 83 (1974): 435. John Searle notes "the leading problem in the biological sciences is the problem of explaining how neurobiological processes cause conscious experiences." John Searle, "The Mystery of Consciousness: Part II," *New York Review of Books* (16 Nov. 1995), 61. Moving from purely naturalistic, unconscious processes to the existence of consciousness appears far more awkward than consciousness' deriving from an ultimate, conscious Being.

[5] *Atheism: A Philosophical Justification* (Philadelphia: Temple Univ. Press, 1991), 106.

[6] In *The Existence of God*, ed. John Hick, (New York: Collier, 1964), 175.

[7] Paul Davies, "Physics and the Mind of God," *First Things* (August/September 1995), 32.

[8] As physicist Paul Davies says, "There is not a shred of evidence that the universe is logically necessary." See his "Physics and the Mind of God," *First Things* (August/September 1995), 32.

[9] Or, on the other hand, it may simply expand indefinitely, during which time its energy is being dissipated.

[10] It is important to remember that this argument does not assume God's existence and then tries to prove it (which is a circular argument). Now when we say that something that begins to exist (like the Big Bang) cannot spontaneously come from nothing, we are not saying that science proves God's existence. We are only saying that the beginning of the universe implies a non-contingent cause of the universe—an inductive conclusion.

[11] See Stephen T. Davis, "The Cosmological Argument and the Epistemic Status of Belief in God," *Philosophia Christi* NS 1/1 (1999): 5-15.

12 Brandon Carter, "Large Number Coincidences and the Anthropic Principle in Cosmology" in M.S. Longair, ed., *Confrontation of Cosmological Theories with Observational Data* (Dordrecht: D. Reidel, 1974), 72.

[13] John Leslie, "The Prerequisites of Life in Our Universe," *Truth* 3 (1991): 99.

[14] Ibid., 102.

[15] John D. Barrow and Joseph Silk, *The Left Hand of Creation* (New York: Oxford Univ. Press, 1993), 227.

[16] Ibid., 26.

[17] Ibid., 227.

[18] Ibid., 38.

[19] Freeman Dyson, "Energy in the Universe," *Scientific American* 225 (Sept. 1971), 25.

[20] John Leslie, *Universes* (London, Routledge, 1989), 1.

[21] Freeman Dyson, "Energy in the Universe," *Scientific American* 225 (Sept. 1971), 25. For further elaboration on the universe's fine-tuning, see Walter Bradley's essay in volume 2 of this series.

[22] Immanuel Kant, *Critique of Practical Reason*, trans. Lewis Beck (N.Y.: Bobbs-Merrill, 1956), 166.

[23] Francis Crick, *The Astonishing Hypothesis: The Scientific Search for the Soul* (New York: Charles Scribner's Sons, 1994), 3.

[24] Taken from Os Guinness, *The Dust of Death* (Downers Grove, IL: InterVarsity Press, 1973), 223.

[25] Kai Nielsen, *Ethics Without God*, rev. ed. (Buffalo, New York: Prometheus Books, 1990), pp. 10-11.

[26] Recounted in *Love Your God With All Your Mind* (Colorado Springs: Navpress, 1997), 153-54.

[27] Or think of the example of *different political systems*. Just because many exist and have existed throughout history and that we happen to grow up in a particular political system doesn't mean that we can't assert that much in, say, Western democracy is far superior to Hitler's dictatorial regime or Stalin's oppressive rule.

[28] Ned Block, "Consciousness" in Samuel Guttenplan, ed., *A Companion to the Philosophy of Mind* (Malden, Mass.: Blackwell, 1994), 211.

[29] Colin McGinn, *The Problem of Consciousness* (Oxford: Basil Blackwell, 1990), 10-11.

[30] McGinn, *The Mysterious Flame: Consciousness Minds in a Material World* (New York: Basic Books, 1999).

[31] Paul Moser, *Why Isn't God More Obvious? Finding the God Who Hides and Seeks* (Atlanta: Ravi Zacharias International Ministries, 2000).

[32] Dallas Willard, "Language, Being, God, and the Three Stages of Theistic Evidence," in J. P. Moreland and Kai Nielsen, *Does God Exist? The Great Debate* (Nashville: Thomas Nelson, 1990), 207.

[33] For further elaboration on this theme, see the introduction in Paul Copan and Paul K. Moser, *The Rationality of Theism* (London: Routledge, forthcoming).

[34] *Pensées* (#429).

[35] Jeremiah 29:13-14.